Enchantment of America
PACIFIC SHORES
The Pacific States

(One in a series of eight books)

Within these five states there is almost everything, ever-frozen tundra, sub-tropical isles, fertile valleys, deserts, rugged mountains and forests of giant trees. But Alaska, California, Hawaii, Oregon, Washington all share the beauty of the Pacific, use its sea lanes and benefit from its trade winds or warm currents.

Here is the dramatic story of the formation of this land and the rhythm of change that has made it what it is.

The first people come—the Seed Gatherers, Northern Fishermen, Aleuts and Eskimos, Polynesians.

Explorers from Mexico leave their mark. Men search for the Northwest Passage. Russians trap furs and claim the land. Sir Francis Drake, Lewis and Clark, Captain Cook, missionaries, fur traders, gold seekers come. Here is this enchanting land today, reflecting varied cultures, customs, art traditons; people making good use of the land's rich resources.

Caves, canyons, forests, volcanoes, ancient ice and tropical splendor may be seen in National Parks and Monuments.

A great book for any traveler in the Pacific states.

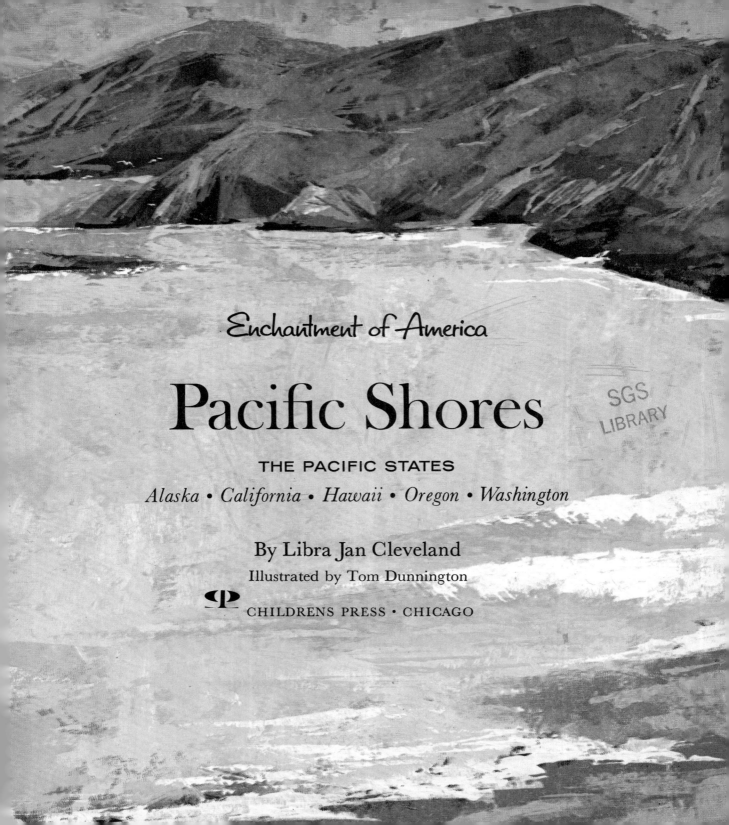

Enchantment of America

Pacific Shores

THE PACIFIC STATES

Alaska • California • Hawaii • Oregon • Washington

By Libra Jan Cleveland

Illustrated by Tom Dunnington

CP CHILDRENS PRESS • CHICAGO

Educational Consultant for the
Enchantment of America Series:
Marilyn M. Spore, Laboratory School,
University of Chicago

Regional Consultant for PACIFIC SHORES:
Charles M. Gates, Ph.D., Professor of History,
University of Washington,
Seattle, Washington

Library of Congress Catalog Card Number: 62-9071

Contents

The Land—prehistory to present

Location

The Pacific Ocean gives miles of rugged and enchanting beauty to California, Oregon and Washington. These three states extend along the western seacoast from Canada to Mexico.

The Pacific surrounds Hawaii, our most southern state, which is about 2,400 miles southwest of the mainland. The peninsula of Alaska, our most northern and our biggest state, reaches out into the Pacific with its southern shore.

All of these states share the beauty that the Pacific gives them.

They are all blessed in some way by its winds and its currents. The trade winds caress the islands of Hawaii. A cool current that flows like a river through the sea keeps Hawaii from being as hot as it would be otherwise. A drift of warm ocean water moderates much of what might be cold climate on the northwest mainland and along the island-dotted southern coast of Alaska.

Our five Pacific states are indebted to the sea in several ways. They all share its beauty, its bounty, and its sea lanes.

Formation and Change

These states related by the Pacific have not always been as we know them now. They were born from the sea. Over some three billion years of geologic time, land forms came into being.

9

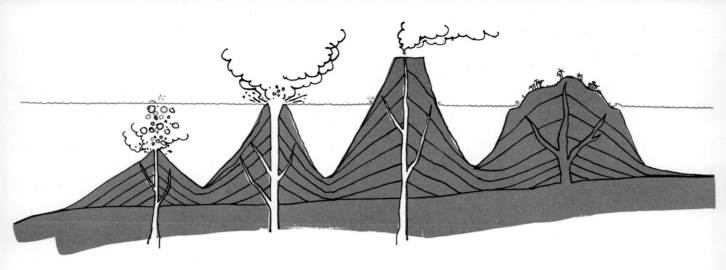

Volcanic Islands

The Hawaiian Islands are the highest tops of a long range of under-sea mountains.

Late in geologic time, volcanoes began erupting along a two-thousand-mile-long crack in the ocean floor. As lava built up, under-sea mountains were formed. It is a long, long story of dome-like peaks rising above the sea to make islands, disappearing and rising again.

From their earliest beginnings, these volcanic mountains began to change. Wind, water and ice went to work on them. Wind and water cut beds for streams in their steep slopes. Earthquakes shook part of them into the sea leaving sharp cliffs. Weather smoothed the roughness of the uplands. Moisture-laden trade winds dropped warm rains on the windward sides of the mountains. Plants began to flourish, and in time, the low warm valleys between the volcanoes became semi-tropical wonderlands.

Ocean waves washed away part of the land and laid it back on the beaches in billions of tiny grains of sand.

Many of the islands are fringed with reefs of coral, built up by the skeletons of the little sea animals.

The parental volcanoes are very much a part of the Hawaiian Islands. Some are still active. Others have been extinct for years. One has a lava lake into which its peak has collapsed. One rises about 14,000 feet above sea level. But measuring from the ocean floor, it rises 32,000 feet, making it the highest mountain in the world.

10

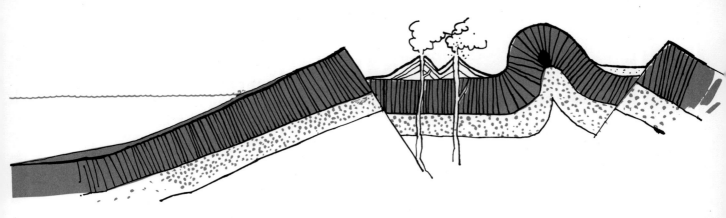

Pacific Borderlands

The ocean pounds along the cliffs, bays and beaches of the Pacific borderlands. Inland lie the sheltered valleys, rugged mountains, and small, isolated plains. The great, green Valley of California is enclosed by the mountains of the Coast Ranges and those of the high, inland, snow-peaked Sierra Nevada Range.

The Sierra Nevadas were born when vast disturbances and the resulting great pressures within the earth caused a massive slab of granite to crack, shift, and fault. The fractured granite tilted skyward in the range's series of jagged peaks that tip toward the ocean. The Sierra Nevadas are part of the great Pacific mountain system that reaches from Panama to Alaska.

The mountains that line the coast are composed of limestone, shale, and sandstone. These sedimentary rocks, laid down in shallow seas, were lifted skyward by other great disturbances far beneath the earth's surface.

Volcanoes and great sheets of lava covered parts of the sea-born layers and helped form the mountains of the Cascade Range. The lava flows spread out again and again until a great plateau 8,000 feet high was built up. The towering, cone-shaped peaks of the Cascades were built up on this platform by layers of outpouring lava and the explosive eruptions of new volcanoes. The Cascades are very new, as geologic time goes. Only about sixty years ago Mount Lassen, in northern California, poured out another layer of lava to add to the vast sheets laid down long before.

11

The Cascade Mountains, too, are part of the Pacific mountain chain, as are the peaks of the mighty Alaska Range, far to the north. The main spur of the crescent of the Alaska Range reaches over into the Aleutian Islands.

Polar Peninsula

The peninsula of Alaska reaches out into the Bering Sea toward Asia. At one point only fifty-five miles of water separate Asia from North America.

Glaciers, frozen, moving masses of ice and snow, are still at work. Some are forty miles long and a thousand feet thick.

Alaska's Mount McKinley, the highest mountain above sea level in the United States, rises 20,300 feet into the sky.

Rhythm of Change

The climate, too, changed with the rhythm of the centuries. The warm, moist Age of Reptiles was followed by the Ice Age. Sheets of ice moved down over the land from the frozen north, retreated and came again. Icebergs floated in Puget Sound, the sheltered inland sea between the coast and the Cascades. Glacial ice ground out the great, broad U-shaped valley of Yosemite.

The climate grew warmer. Melting ice swelled the ocean and the waters rose to cover coastal lowlands with shallow seas.

Then the waters receded.

The Willamette and Lower Columbia Valley received layers of rich sediment from the sea that covered them.

The Gulf of California drew back, leaving behind the rich, fertile Imperial Valley.

What was once a tropical forest settled under the water of an inland sea. Then this, the Mojave Valley, was shaken up again above the water by violent volcanic action.

13

A great volcanic peak of the Cascades, Mount Mazama, exploded. As the eruptions increased in violence, the prehistoric peak's cinder cone sank and the great volcano collapsed.

The Klamath Indians of the region have a legend that tells of this violent geologic episode. The area around near-by Mount Shasta was regarded as the battleground of the gods and when Mount Mazama fell, this terrible and mystifying occurrence was looked upon as an awesome chapter in the war of the gods. Mount Mazama was regarded as the home of a powerful god and the great explosion signified this god's defeat and the destruction of his towering throne. The legend of the terrible war grew, perhaps, from the accounts handed down through many generations by the few survivors who witnessed the fiery destruction. When the first white men came to the region, they found that the Indians still would not venture near this ancient, awesome battleground of the gods.

Many ancient, pumice-covered Indian relics found in caves throughout central Oregon tell another part of the tale. They prove, indeed, that there were Indians who saw the fall of the mighty Mount Mazama.

While the legend of the fiery fall of the great Mount Mazama grew, the rains fell. Slowly the old crater, sunken far below the shattered rim, filled with water. A deep, blue lake, the sixth deepest in the world, was formed. This beautiful lake was to be called Crater Lake. A small, secondary cone built its way up from the bottom of the deep parent crater through the water. This small, new volcano, with just the top of its smooth cone reaching above the cold, blue waters of Crater Lake, is Wizard Isle.

Change Is Constant

Peaks and prairies, lakes and lowlands are not all born by violence. Change is constant. Through the ages, the very forces of nature at work today were responsible for the shaping and shifting of the earth's surface. Jagged peaks of newly risen mountain ranges were softened, smoothed and polished by wind, rain and ice. Rushing streams grew into mighty rivers, cutting out deep canyons and wide valleys, building up plains with soil stolen from the mountains. Scientists read the long story of the earth's formation and change from the rocks and fossils of the land.

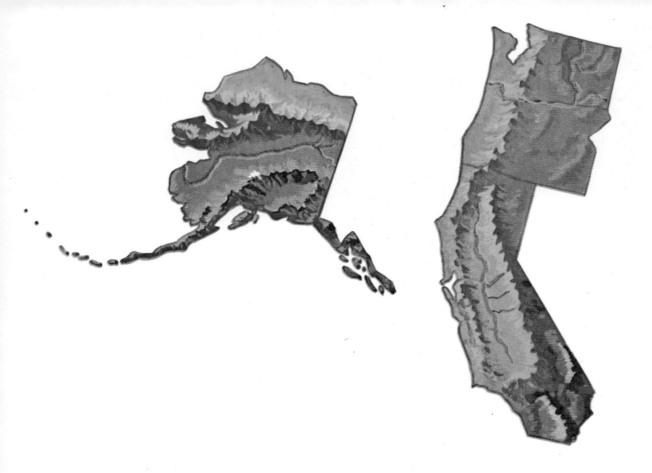

Lay of the Land Today

Volcanoes, glaciers, earthquakes, the restless sea and millions of years of erosion have left a heritage of wonder in the Pacific States. What other small group of states can boast of arctic tundra as well as semi-tropical jungles? Where else do snow-capped mountains look down on a Death Valley 282 feet below sea level? Where else will you find, within a few miles, a sheltered seacoast, a fertile valley, a hot desert or a snow-capped mountain? Surprisingly close together are tumbling waterfalls, jeweled lakes, polished granite domes, deep canyons, sandy beaches, and redwood forests.

There are wooded, rain-drenched coastal slopes, timbered mountains, and rolling farm and pasture lands.

Mountains, valleys, plateaus and rivers make ribbed and rickracked patterns across the land.

16

Alaska is divided horizontally by mountains into three major regions. North of the Brooks Range, the tundra, the flat, treeless plain, reaches into the arctic. Between the Brooks Range and the Alaska Range in the south there is the vast central valley of Alaska through which the Yukon River flows to the Bering Sea. The river is still the main artery of transportation through this rugged country. South of the Alaska Range, sheltered by it from the north and mellowed by the Japan Current in the sea, is the temperate coastline country.

Between the Coast Ranges and the Cascades of Washington and Oregon is the fertile Willamette-Puget Sound Valley. Beyond the Cascades to the east, the Columbia Plateau rises toward the Rocky Mountains.

The Columbia and the Willamette rivers join to form a part of the Oregon-Washington boundary line, then, flow into the Pacific.

California has its Coastal Ranges on the west and the high ridge of the Sierra Nevadas on the east, with the great Central Valley of California between them. The Sacramento River from the north and the San Joaquin River from the south meet and flow through the Coast Ranges into San Francisco Bay.

The once barren volcanic mountain tops that form the Hawaiian Islands have been sculptured by erosion and clothed in sub-tropical splendor until this state is now called "The Paradise of the Pacific."

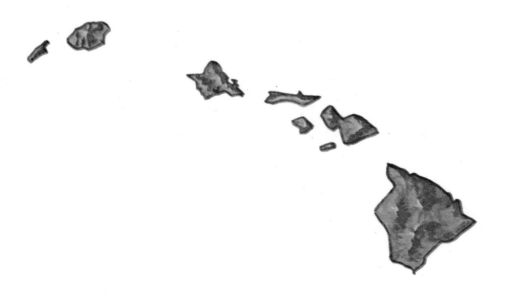

Climate

The climate of the Pacific States is as varied as the land forms.

The land of the treeless tundra of Alaska's arctic region has been frozen solid for thousands of years. Winters there are long and cold. Summers are short, cool and cloudy.

Alaska's central valley has an extreme range of temperature, from perhaps 78 degrees below zero in the winter to 90 degrees above zero in the summer.

The climate of the southern coastal region, tempered by the Japan Current is mild and wet. Temperatures seldom go below zero.

Washington and Oregon have a mild, wet climate along the coast. Here, rain forests hold centuries of wetness.

Rain-bearing clouds skim over the low coastal mountains into the Willamette-Puget Sound Valley. A warm ocean current keeps the Valley from being too hot in the summer or too cold in the winter.

Between the Cascade Mountains and the Rockies, the high Columbia Plateau gets a little rain during mild winters. But in the hot dry summers, the many crops depend upon irrigation for water.

California has a comfortable, mild climate along the seacoast but the long Central Valley is cut off from rain by the high coastal mountains. Rain and snow on the western slopes of the Sierras feed many streams that run through the Valley. The northern part of the Valley is temperate. The southern part is so warm that semi-tropical fruits can be grown.

The San Bernardino Valley in southern California is not cut off from the rain clouds and it has almost a year-round growing season.

The Imperial Valley in southeastern California has a subtropical climate and, here, too, thanks to a fine irrigation system, crops can be grown throughout the year.

There are several hot, dry desert areas in California which may someday be turned into farm lands by irrigation.

The gentle climate of Hawaii remains constant with the help of the cool drift of the Bering Current and the trade winds. There is heavy rainfall on the windward side of the mountains. Having dropped their moisture, the warm dry winds blow across leaving arid and semi-arid regions on the far sides of the mountains.

19

The First People

The formation of the land, thought of in terms of geologic time, took about three billion years. So, in view of this, it was quite recently that the first people came to this continent about twenty-five thousand years ago.

There was once a land or ice bridge from the continent of Asia to what is now the Alaskan peninsula. Many scientists think that the first people walked to this continent across that land bridge. Some, perhaps, followed the chain of the Aleutian Islands. This was thousands of years before the time of Christ.

These people were primitive nomads, wandering in search of food. As years passed, they spread slowly over the two American continents. The main stream of this migration flowed south through the valleys into South America. Gradually, groups moved west and east from the valleys until the vast area of North America was thinly settled.

Not much is known about these prehistoric tribes. Picture-writings on basalt rocks in the Columbia Basin may someday tell us more about the aboriginal tribes that once wandered through this region.

As groups settled, the nature of the land, the available food, the climate, all influenced the many ways of living which developed. But no group in North America ever reached the height of civilization achieved by the Incas in South America or the Mayas and Aztecs in Central America and Mexico.

By the time Columbus discovered America and called the natives *Indians* there were about a million of them living in North America. They were separated into several hundred tribes and were speaking about two hundred different languages.

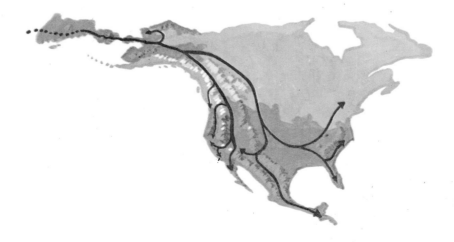

Seed Gatherers

The Spanish explorers found a group of Indians called *Seed Gatherers* living in California. They lived on the nuts, roots and berries of the region and ate shell fish and small game. The Seed Gatherers avoided the big game because of superstitions. The Santa Barbara Channel tribes had plank boats and tools made of bone, stone, shell, and wood.

The houses of these people were brush and bark huts, sometimes earth-covered. They were cone or dome shaped and often they were partially underground. One rude hut housed all of one family, from the old grandparents to the babies.

They did not make pottery or work with metal. They had few religious ceremonies and less government. They lived in family and village groups.

Indians in the northern groups of Seed Gatherers wore straw-basket hats and skin capes to protect them from the rain. They had rabbit-skin robes.

They excelled in basket-making. They wove their baskets with colorful designs, decorated them with shells and used them for everything—hats, storage, and even cooking.

21

Northern Fishermen

The natives north of Humbolt Bay in California and in most of Oregon and Washington represented quite a different culture. They were the *Northern Fishermen*. They ate the fish in the rivers and the sea. They used the cedar logs of the forest to make dugout canoes in which they traveled on the rivers. Some of their large ocean-going canoes could hold sixty men.

They made many uses of the trees of the forest. They built large rectangular houses. A heavy framework of posts and beams was covered by cedar planks which had to be split out with bone, horn or stone wedges. Many families shared a house which was divided inside into family quarters. A ring of stones in the center of the house formed a fireplace. The smoke rose through a hole in the roof.

The posts of the houses had carvings of animal heads on them.

Clothing was often made of shredded cedar bark.

There were many tribes of these Northern Fishermen and they spoke many languages, but their basic culture was much the same. Tribes of this group lived all along the northern coastline of North America up into southeastern Alaska. Among the northern tribes, wood carving became an art and grotesque totem poles told the stories of the clan, and pictured its animal ancestors.

Songs and dances told the stories of the ancient days when animals could talk.

Salmon was the chief food of these Indians. It could be cut in strips and when dried or smoked could be stored in wooden boxes for winter use.

Sometimes the hunters went whaling in a big canoe and shared the catch with the community. The women and children gathered berries and fern shoots. These Indians raised no food and there were taboos against eating the flesh of some land animals.

The women were expert weavers and wove beautiful blankets from the hair of dogs and mountain goats.

Aleuts and Eskimos

The Aleuts, living on the chain of islands sweeping southwest from Alaska, were related to the Eskimos by language. The name Eskimo means "eater of raw meat." They developed a way of living which made survival possible in a rugged climate.

Eskimos had settled along the arctic coasts in small family or tribal groups without a chief. In the absence of wood, they used skin to make several different types of boats. Tents were made of skin too. Some huts were built of stone, partially underground for warmth. Sometimes they were built with blocks of snow.

Polynesians

There were primitive people on the continent of North America for thousands of years before anyone came to the Hawaiian Islands. These islands are a part of a far-flung group of islands called *Polynesia*. The word means "many islands." People from the southernmost of these islands were the first to come to Hawaii.

The Polynesians were tall, handsome people. They lived well on fish, berries, and roots. They raised pigs and chickens. They made rope from coconut fiber and tied their grass houses together skillfully. They had no metal, but they used shell, bone, and stone for tools and fishhooks. They were magnificent seamen and could navigate their outrigger canoes over thousands of miles of ocean with only the stars to guide them. Some of these canoes could hold a hundred people and all of their goods and pigs and chickens.

It was one such group as this that came first to the Hawaiian Islands. When Captain Cook discovered the islands, he found about 250,000 Polynesian natives living there.

What dramatic earth forces helped form the Pacific States?

In what ways do winds, ocean currents and mountains affect climate in the Pacific lands?

How do we know that fertile valleys were once under water?

How did the sea and the forests contribute to the ways in which the ancient Eskimos and Aleuts, the Northern Fishermen, the Seed Gatherers and the Polynesians lived?

25

People come from many lands

Explorers from Mexico

Less than fifty years after Columbus made his famous voyage from Spain and found a new continent blocking his way to the riches of the Indies, Mexico City had risen on the ruins of the ancient Aztec capital of Tenochitlán. This was newly acquired territory for the King of Spain and he grew curious about the lands to the north. Explorers in the service of the king were sent north by land and sea.

In 1540, Hernando de Alarcón found the Colorado River and made his way up it to the north and became the first white man to set foot in the wonderful country bordered by the Pacific.

Two years later, Juan Rodrigues Cabrillo set sail for the north with two ships.

This little sea party sailed along the coast, landed several times, visited with the friendly Indians, and claimed the land in the name of the Spanish king.

About the same time, Bartolome Ferrelo sailed as far as what is now southern Oregon in search of the Northwest Passage.

The Spanish names that dot the coastline of the Pacific remain as tributes to these early sea voyagers.

The Northwest Passage

A great treasure hunt was underway for a water route across the American continent. The idea persisted that the American continent was merely something to be crossed on the way to the riches of the Indies and the Orient. Rumors of a Northwest Passage led to exploration of the coast lands throughout the next two hundred years.

England's Sir Francis Drake

Great Britain's attempt at locating the fabled passage brought the famed *Golden Hind* and her captain, Sir Francis Drake, to the shores of the Pacific. Drake landed briefly near what is now San Francisco, and claimed the land for his queen, Elizabeth I, forty years before the Pilgrims landed on the other side of the continent.

When Drake's company continued north along the coast and on to complete the first English voyage around the world, they left behind a gold plaque to prove Drake's claim to the coastlands. More than three hundred years later, this plaque was found buried in the sand near the spot where the *Golden Hind* had been beached.

Drake's visit aroused the authorities in Madrid and Mexico to strengthen the Spanish hold on these northern lands. Two expeditions were sent to explore the California coast and the off-shore islands. Capes, bays and other landmarks still have the names given them by these Spanish explorers who came by sea.

During the next hundred years there was little exploration of the Pacific lands. The search for the Northwest Passage was all but forgotten.

Wars at home prevented further exploration under the flag of Spain.

The English were concentrating on the settlement of the eastern seaboard of the American continent. The restriction of civil and religious liberties, civil war, and a growing discontent in the British Isles sent people to America's east coast to establish new homes. England was also involved in wars at home and in Europe and suffered from the plague.

Charles II of England granted a charter, in 1670, to "The Company of Adventurers of England Trading into Hudson's Bay" to discover a new passage to the South Seas and to trade in furs. But no English adventurers reached the Pacific Coast until more than a hundred years later.

The powers of Europe were much too busy with affairs at home to bother with the wilds of the far Pacific lands.

Russians on the Coastlands

Peter the Great of Russia was not too busy at home to take an interest in the coast lands of the North American continent. He wanted to know more about the relation of Siberia to the New World. He considered taking possession of territories not yet occupied in North America. The Danish explorer, Vitus Bering, was sent by the Russians to investigate the land along the cold northwest coast.

In 1728 Bering sailed far enough north, through what is now called the Bering Strait, to conclude that Alaska was indeed separated from Siberia. Less than twenty years later, Bering made a second voyage which took him to the Alaskan coast. He died on the homeward journey but his crew brought back to Russia glowing reports of the great herds of fur-bearing animals they had seen.

Russia then took possession of Alaska and established there a profitable trade in sea-otter skins.

Maritime Fur Traders

The age of the Maritime Fur Traders had begun and would flourish for a hundred years.

Russian fur traders in great numbers advanced along the Alaskan off-shore islands and all but cleared the country of furs. The sea otters were almost exterminated. Aleutian natives were enslaved. The Indians fought the intruders.

Spurred by Russian reports of Alaskan fur wealth, British traders sailed up and down North America's western coastline trading trinkets for furs. Then, sailing across the Pacific, they traded the furs for the gold, silks, and sandalwood of the Orient.

Spanish Mission Lands

Disturbed by Russian and British advances, Spain took a renewed interest in the shorelands north of Mexico. In 1769 four expeditions were dispatched from Mexico to establish permanent settlements that would strengthen Spanish claims to the land.

Don Gaspar de Portolá and his small band moved up the coast from the first mission settlement at San Diego. He was accompanied by a Franciscan monk, Father Junípero Serra. Under his guidance a string of twenty-one missions from San Diego to Sonoma was built during the next fifty years. These missions were spaced just one good day's journey apart. This path of the padres and the missions was *El Camino Real,* the King's Way. Today this mission-dotted route is a modern highway bearing the old Spanish name as well as a route number.

Portolá continued up the coast to find the site of what is now San Francisco. Less than ten years later, the first ship sailed through the Golden Gate into the bay that Sir Frances Drake had missed when he sailed by, two hundred years before.

By 1776 a force of Spanish soldiers was stationed at the Presidio in San Francisco, which is today the United States 6th Army Headquarters.

Voyages to the North

The great fortunes in furs made by the Russian traders sent the Spanish far to the north. Spanish seamen sailed to Alaska's southeast coast.

Other nations, too, led by the gleam of riches and glory, sent expeditions to the polar peninsula.

England's Captain James Cook made extensive surveys along the Alaskan coast. This was after his discovery of what he called the Sandwich Islands, which lay halfway between Alaska and Australia.

Captain Cook and the Sandwich Islands

The group of sub-tropical islands in the midst of the Pacific, named by Captain Cook in 1778 for England's Earl of Sandwich, were the eight main islands of what is now the state of Hawaii.

Captain Cook returned to the Islands late that same year. He was greeted by the nephew of the chief of the island of Hawaii. However, his stay of several months was brought to an end by his sudden death, caused by "unfortunate incidents ashore." He was murdered.

Within less than twenty years, Kamehameha, the nephew of Hawaii's chief made himself master of this island and dominated or conquered all but two of the others. The year 1795 saw this "Napoleon of the Pacific" defeat his rivals and enemies and unite the islands into one kingdom. This was the beginning of the dynasty that ruled the Hawaiian Islands for a hundred years.

Americans Sail the Pacific

Soon after Captain Cook's last trip, the flourishing fur trade with China, the beginnings of the Hawaiian sandalwood trade, and the great age of whaling brought other visitors to the islands.

The first American ships sailed into one of the many island bays just ten years after Cook's fatal visit.

When Captain Robert Gray anchored his ship, *Columbia*, near one of the islands, he was on his way to the Orient. He had been trading and exploring along a great part of North America's Pacific coastline.

Three years later he was back again on America's northwest coast. This time he sailed into the mouth of the "great river that runs to the sea." named it after his ship, the *Columbia,* and established a claim to the Pacific Northwest for the United States.

Lewis and Clark Come Overland

The success of the maritime fur traders encouraged overland expeditions to the coastlands.

Lewis and Clark were sent by President Jefferson to explore and map the unknown country between Missouri and Oregon. They reached the shores of the Pacific in 1805 after a long and perilous journey over the mountains and down the Columbia River. In their reports to the government they told of this land so rich in furs.

Fur Trading Heyday

John Jacob Astor, a successful New York merchant, had made a fortune in furs and he was interested in this report of new fur country. He sent a large expedition to the mouth of the Columbia River, and a fur-trading post was set up at Astoria, Oregon.

Soon the great northwest fur trade was in its heyday and bitter rivalry flared between competing companies. Through merger and acquisition, John Jacob Astor's Pacific Fur Company, The Hudson's Bay Company and the North West Company of Canada dominated the land. The fur companies controlled the whole region west of the Rockies from Alaska to California.

Trading posts dotted the coastlands and company hunters and trappers explored the region thoroughly in their search for furs. These fur-hunting trail blazers gave names to many of the streams, lakes and mountains

The Russian-American Company dominated the Alaskan fur trade and began to settle this barren land. Sitka, soon the most cosmopolitan town west of the Mississippi and north of Mexico City, became the capital. Russian-Orthodox wood-frame churches with turnip-shaped tops were built by the Aleuts and Indians under the guidance of Russian missionaries.

The southern-most Russian outpost was set up near San Francisco. Fort Ross protected the settlers from the Indians and soon the town-fort of Bodega was in business as a fur-trading post and mission. The Russian settlers began to raise sloes for vodka, and apples.

Further south, exploration by Indian scouts and soldiers of fortune, and three expeditions led by General John Charles Frémont pointed the westward way into the golden valley of California.

The Florida Treaty of 1819 with the Spanish gave the United States "any and all rights" claimed by Spain to the northwest country. England and the United States held the land jointly, by agreement, until 1846. At that time the 49th parallel was established as the boundary between Canada and the United States.

The Oregon Trail

People began to think of the northwest country as something more than fur country. Missionaries coming west to serve the Indians followed the old path taken by hunters and trappers. Families with tools and household goods packed across South Pass following a trail that led over the Rocky Mountains to Oregon.

It was a perilous trip from Fort Boise, in Idaho, to the Oregon Dalles, and it had to be made on foot or by horseback. Marcus Whitman, a missionary, was determined to take a wagon over this trail. He and his wife were on their way, in the company of another missionary couple, to minister to the Oregon Indians. As the rough journey progressed, the wagon was reduced to a cart, and finally, only the wheels were left. But Marcus Whitman did get his wheels to Oregon, on the back of a pack mule. By 1836 the little party had established a mission near Walla Walla.

Later, many covered wagons successfully made the journey and the old game trail grew wide and deeply rutted with use. Some of the people in search of new homes followed a branch of this trail south, into the Valley of California.

Traders and hardy homesteaders reaching California found that the government of newly independent Mexico had divided this vast land into some seven hundred great estates and had distributed these estates, or *ranchos,* to prominent citizens and their families.

In spite of this, some of the American settlers obtained land grants from Mexico and stayed to settle in the great, fertile Valley of California.

Missionaries Reach Hawaii

As early missionaries headed overland to the wilds of the Oregon Coast, other missionaries sailed from Eastern sea ports to the "paradise" of the Hawaiian Islands.

The whalers and trading ships that had anchored in the island harbors brought diseases, common to white men, but deadly to the susceptible islanders. Soon the native population would be all but non-existent. The early missionaries had their work cut out for them.

After long, arduous voyages, often by way of stormy and dangerous Cape Horn, many missionary families reached the islands. They brought not only Christian teachings to the islanders, but new customs and the first written native language as well. Many of the first missionary families stayed and became instrumental in the development of a new, western way of life for the islands.

Gold

In 1848 flakes of gold, discovered in the waters of Captain Sutter's sawmill in California's Sierra foothills, added to the lure of furs and fertile lands. Gold focused the world's attention on this remote frontier and transformed it into a land where hordes of miners sifted gravel in foothill streams in search of gleaming treasure.

Bustling supply towns came into existence, virtually overnight. Once deserted seaports echoed daily with the shouts of newly arrived seekers of the golden wealth. The gold rush hastened the development of the region and brought about in a matter of months what would have taken many years to accomplish under normal conditions.

Towns sprang up from one end of the new state of California to the other. Sleepy, Spanish-Mexican settlements such as San Francisco (formerly *Yerba Buena*) became busy American cities. San Francisco mushroomed. At the end of one year's time there were twelve times as many people as there had been. This fantastic growth often brought trouble along with the people. In one year alone, there was an average of a murder a day. Lynch-law and the vigilantes were, for a time, the only law and order to be had. The over-expanded, rapidly and poorly built town was swept by fire six times in these early days. But the real disaster came in 1863 when a terrible drought hit the region, sharply reducing the already badly strained food supplies.

The gold rush brought new life to the other coastal lands. It furnished an ever-growing market for the lumber and flour produced further north. Steamboats paddled busily through the waters of the upper Columbia carrying supplies to miners. Ocean-going vessels sailed from Portland to San Francisco.

Late in the 1890's, another gold rush lured people to the Pacific lands. This time the rush was far to the north, to the Canadian Yukon. Alaska's near-by Nome and Klondike, once thought to be nothing but barren waste lands, proved to be rich in gold, too. Adventurous sourdoughs from all over the world headed for the Alaskan wilds. In their wake came merchants who could be sure of getting the gold as fast as the sourdoughs could find it by supplying goods and services at sky-high prices.

And so as the once profitable fur trade declined, new sources of income—agriculture and mining, barter and business, found their places in the rapidly growing economy of the Pacific lands.

Things to think about

In what ways are we still reminded of the Spanish explorers?

Why did so many of the first explorers come to the West Coast by sea?

What made people of many countries look upon the search for the Northwest Passage as a treasure hunt?

How did other things besides furs lead to the settlement of the Pacific lands?

39

Life on Pacific Shores today

Natural Wealth

Hunters, traders, missionaries, people in search of new homes, people in search of wealth came to the Pacific's shores.

They found fertile valleys, great rivers that ran to the sea, favorable climates for living and growing. Here was water teeming with fish; water for navigation, for crops, for power. Rugged mountains with lush forests offered strong-fibered wood, enough and more for homes, bridges and cities. The mountains held mineral wealth, formed within them centuries before. Vast range lands for cattle and sheep were here beside the sun-warmed valleys and plateaus that would nurture grains, fruits and vegetables. Here was land, soil, climate, and water for a good today and a better tomorrow.

Agriculture, industry, recreation, power, and daily life all require vast amounts of water. And from earliest times man has used the waterways as highways from one place to another.

All over the world, water is one of the most valuable natural resources. From the waters of the seas came life. Without water, life cannot exist. Even in the states bordered by the great Pacific, water, though plentiful in most places, is precious. It must be used wisely.

Glaciers, snowfields, rainfall, running rivers, high peaks that capture moisture-bearing clouds, cap rocks that seal great underground wells are all potential sources of life-giving water. Man is learning how to find and use this wealth of water wisely and well.

Huge dams and reservoirs have been built to store water. Men learned what kind of rock stored water and then drilled deep wells to find it. Men learned how to irrigate dry lands by bringing water to them in pipes and ditches.

In many places, the available water is being used up. There is a new awareness of the need to avoid waste and at the same time, to find and use new sources. The ocean itself may prove to be a valuable source. Several experimental processes that take the salt out of the water are being tried.

Fish, Farm and Ranch Riches

The Pacific States have always shared the bounty of the sea. From earliest times, the peoples of the coasts and islands relied upon it for food and transportation. Late-comers to the ocean lands, too, made use of the gifts of the sea.

Fishing continues to be one of the major pursuits in these lands. Commercial fishing crews take tons of salmon, halibut, cod, sturgeon, herring, tuna, sardines and many varieties of shellfish from Pacific waters each year.

The fertile, black earth of the river valleys, enriched by the waters; the acid, red dirt of the islands, rich with lava; the frozen tundra lands of the north that hide mineral treasure—all have held promise for man since they were laid down millions of years ago.

Indians of the coastlands gathered seeds, wild berries and ferns.

The people of the Hawaiian islands raised beds of *taro* to make *poi*. Today lush fields of sugar cane, pineapple, coffee, grains and vegetables have taken their place on the land. Some of the first white families that went to Hawaii started to use land, unfit for raising sugar or pineapple, for grazing land. Today one of the largest ranches in the world is Hawaii's Parker Ranch where *paniolos,* Hawaiian cowboys, ride the 275,000 acre range.

The open plains of the Pacific States have been used for cattle raising since Spanish-Mexican days.

Wool and meat from sheep ranches and milk products from dairy herds come from green mainland valleys.

Mineral and Timber Treasures

Treasure stores of minerals waited in the depths of ice-clad mountains and far under the ocean to be brought to the surface.

When California was admitted to the Union, its major industry was mining. Gold was king. But in less time than it takes for a tall tree to stretch high, the king of the mountains, plains and shores was black gold, oil, and its crown prince was natural gas.

The mineral wealth of our last frontier, Alaska, is still to be fully explored. But the gold, platinum, copper and tin that have been found in valuable quantities hold promise for the future.

For almost ninety years Oregon has had an interest in gold although the output has not been large. Now, building minerals, sand, stone, and gravel are a major part of this state's mineral production. Oregon has the only producing nickel mine in the United States.

Gold, copper, lead and zinc, in moderate quantities, come from Washington. Beds of limestone and other building materials are quarried in Hawaii.

The vast forests of Washington and Oregon make lumbering the most important industry in these two states. Much of the lumber in the United States comes from the rainy, wet mountains of this region.

Washington and Oregon are famous for their ponderosa pine and magnificent stands of Douglas fir that cover the damp coastal ranges. California's ancient, towering redwoods are not only beautiful tourist attractions, but are widely used for building materials.

Alaska is proud of her production of hemlock, spruce and cedar.

The native hardwoods in Hawaii, *koa* and monkey pod, as well as eucalyptus, are used in many products. One day the volcano-top forests of the islands may prove to be a most valuable asset, since Hawaiian timber grows two to three times faster than mainland varieties.

Lumber, shingles, fuel, pulp, furniture, houses—many thousands of things, come from the deep dark forests of the Pacific States.

Manufacturing and Processing

Raw materials, if they are to be used fully, must be gathered, processed and distributed.

Throughout the Pacific States, lumber mills, oil refineries, ore smelteries, food-processing plants, chemical and woodworking operations convert raw materials into widely usable products.

The first commercial cannery was set up on the Columbia River as early as 1866 to preserve and distribute the great supplies of salmon available in the area.

Refining and foundry operations were started to convert raw mineral ores into materials for new and growing industries. From these and other points come materials for building, manufacturing and processing, and transportation; materials to build a region and a country. Steel, aluminum, fuel, ceramics, airplanes, medicines, intricate electronic mechanisms, food products in all imaginable forms, textiles, and many more such products come from the Pacific States.

Transportation

Expansion and growth of a region depend on adequate ways to move goods and raw materials from source to processor, to consumer. In the Pacific States, railroads, highways, steamships and airlines came to link the region with other parts of the country and other parts of the world. Railroads stretched across the continent; river ports and deep-water ocean harbors invited trade; bridges leap-frogged islands, rivers, and bays to help speed products to people and to promote the growth and development of the region.

The many modes of transportation in the Pacific States contribute to one of this region's most important businesses—serving tourists. The natural and man-made wonders of the area attract people from far and wide. Transportation brings them to the Pacific lands.

Communications

One of the tourist attractions of the region is the vast realm of the movie and television industries in California. Movies and television are one of the most recent forms of mass communication.

Communication has been a very important factor in the region's development from primitive wilderness to a busy, modern complex of cities and industries.

Ancient Indian tribes painted pictures on rocks and later carefully carved totem poles. They were passing along information to others. This is communication; the sending and receiving of a message. Later Indians and the Polynesians of Hawaii used drums to send messages. When explorers and trappers blazed trees along the trails, they were leaving a message: "This is the way."

As more people came to the region, faster, more easily understood methods of communication developed. Stagecoach and mail rider, the telegraph, all carried messages. Newspapers and letters put aboard ocean-going vessels or tucked in a saddlebag brought news to faraway places. But by the time news was received, it was weeks, months, or even years old. Now telephone and telegraph cables, laid under the ocean or strung over mountains and plains, bring news almost instantly.

The People of The Pacific States

The people of the coastlands, the volcanic islands, and the polar peninsula are people of many lands and cultures. They came to the lands of the Pacific for many different reasons.

From Asia came Eskimos, Aleuts, Indians, and Polynesians in search of new homes. From Europe came Spaniards, Russians, French-Canadians and Englishmen, in search of new lands to settle, in search of furs to trade. People came to see, to teach, to live.

The development of sugar and pineapple plantations created a need for labor that could not be met by the dwindling native population of Hawaii. Chinese were brought to the islands to work in the fields. Later other Orientals, Japanese, Koreans, Filipinos were brought to the island fields.

The gold rush brought people to the coastlands. From America's east coast, from China, Mexico, the British Isles, Germany and Russia they came. People came to help the railroads stretch across the continent.

New industries brought new people to the land. Italians, Greeks, Yugoslavs and Japanese manned the fishing fleets. Scandinavians and Finns lumberjacked in the deep forests. Swiss, Portuguese and Armenians contributed their skills to gardening and the growing of fruit.

Some of the people came to stay only a few years and stayed on instead to build new homes and a new life for themselves, their children and their children's children.

The people who came to the Pacific lands turned the mountains inside out; they turned the earth upside down; they built a land of fertile farms, vast industries; a land knit together by railroads, telegraph lines and sea lanes.

People are still coming to the states of the Pacific. The population continues to expand at a tremendous rate. Even though Alaska is still the least populous state in the Union, its population increased 75 per cent during the last ten years. California, one of the most thickly populated states, increased about 50 per cent, and the population of Hawaii grew more than 25 per cent. Population growth in Oregon and Washington helps make the Pacific States one of the fastest growing regions in the nation.

Variegated Cultures, Customs and Art Traditions

Some of the people who came to the lands of the Pacific brought old arts and customs with them. Some of the earliest people had to develop new customs and ways of life to fit their new lands. Out of old lands and old customs, new cultures were born for the new lands.

49

Today, the Eskimos and some of the Indians have preserved the customs, habits and language that their ancestors developed centuries ago. They still live much as their forefathers did before the white men came. They are fur trappers and fishermen, miners, seal-hunters and seamen. The Eskimos are great carvers of ivory obtained from the walrus, and stone.

The Indians of the north regarded trees as their friends. From the great trees the Indians carved many items necessary for daily life. For fun they carved tall, gaily painted totem poles from cedar trees. The totems often told the family history, or of great chiefs, of animals, or special events. The Indians wove baskets from cedar strips and beautiful blankets from bark and mountain-goat wool.

Since these early peoples had no written language, they kept their records by carving totem poles and figures, or by painting and weaving stories into their designs, and by creating dances to commemorate events. Many examples of native weaving, carving and woodworking can be seen today.

Many of the Indians farther south now live on reservations and retain few of their old ways. They work in the forests, or in commercial fishing industries; a number are farmers and stockmen.

Some of the many people who have come to the Pacific States brought with them the customs and crafts of their old homelands. Today the culture of the Pacific lands is a blend of East and West, Orient and Occident. Words, food, and games are a mixture of many cultures and customs.

The relaxed, open-air way of life of the Pacific States has contributed many words, sports, and pleasant pastimes to this region and to the whole country. The *Kaffeeklatsch,* the *patios* and *lanais, rodeos, luaus,* surfboarding and the *hula* are familiar things to most of us.

The architecture of this region reflects many cultures. Stucco buildings tell of the Spanish Mission past. Redwood, used in building, whispers of the forest giants. Homes with Chinese Moon Gates and curved eaves like Japanese pagodas offer invitations to come in. Oriental bamboo furniture and grass mats are in common use. Turnip-topped frame churches are silent reminders of the Russians.

In the old days, the hula was a dance-history of the island people, their ancestors and their deeds. The dance told stories of long voyages, the weather, the shore and sea. Often a new dance would be created for a special occasion such as the visit of an important chief.

Ceremonial dances of the Indians told stories, too. Musical accompaniment for the dances was furnished by songs and chants, drums made of skin, and rattles made from bone or gourds.

These dances, the Chinese Dragon Dance—reminiscent of the Old Orient, romantic ballet from Russia and France, symphonic music, opera and modern forms of dance and music, are all part of the colorful art tradition of the Pacific States.

Drama, too, which evolved from the dance long ago, is a blend of many peoples and times. Impressive ancient Indian ceremonies and pageants, dramas of Shakespeare played out in a theatre patterned after London's 16th century Fortune Theatre, the concept of "theatre in the round," the glamour of movie and television spectaculars are all a part of the Pacific tradition.

Ivory, stone and wood sculptures, beautiful bowls of polished *koa* wood, mats and hats woven or braided from jungle grasses, *leis* made from gorgeous tropical flowers, polished ivory or delicate feathers, *tapa* cloth pounded out from mulberry wood, bright patterns and colors compose some of the many faces of the artful craft tradition of Pacific lands.

We know that man has told of his exploits, his adventures, his feelings in dance, painting, carving, crafts and music for many ages. Not until recently, in terms of man's existence in time, did he learn to record events and impressions in writing.

The Pacific lands have a literary tradition of their own, characteristic of the people, their deeds, their lands. Gold-seeker, teacher and journalist Bret Harte wrote of the wild and rough gold rush days in his stories of *The Luck of Roaring Camp* and *The Outcasts of Poker Flat*. Jack London recorded the primitive power of the cold north lands. Joaquin Miller turned the beauties of the Sierra region into poetry. Robert Louis Stevenson spent much of his life absorbing the essence of the islands and turned his impressions into poetry.

Many threads of tradition are woven into the tapestry of colorful patterns that is the living, growing culture of our Pacific lands.

53

Education and Research — Modern Treasure Hunt

Two hundred years ago, Spanish missionaries built missions along the coastlands and brought Christian teachings to the primitive Indians. They also taught these natives how to grow crops and brought them a better way of life. Since that time, education and a regard for the future have always been valued highly in the Pacific States.

In the early 1800's, other missionaries started the first schools in the Oregon Country for Indian children. Soon free public schools were in operation. Missionaries brought schools and a written language to the people of the islands and the polar peninsula. They taught the natives how to read and how to open the door to a better future for themselves and their children.

The churches founded academies and colleges. The big island plantation owners started private schools. The government established land-grant universities. Day schools, boarding schools, schools for teachers, schools for the children of the Hawaiian nobles soon flourished.

Today, in addition to regular studies, schools, colleges and universities of the Pacific lands sponsor research projects devoted to the particular needs of the region. There are special programs in volcanology, sugar and pineapple technology and marine biology.

Some programs provide opportunities for education and research in the fields of physics of the earth related to the arctic, wildlife, conservation of natural resources, long-range weather forecasting, and geology and minerology.

Much of the land of the Pacific States is a natural laboratory. Agricultural experimental stations develop new methods to increase production of crops and animals, and to promote better utilization of present resources. Through research and experiment, many new uses have been discovered for former waste products of agriculture and industry.

A two-hundred inch reflecting telescope stands atop lofty Mount Palomar in California and another large telescope stands on Mount Wilson, great eyes probing the heavens.

Quakes and tremors far beneath the surface of the earth are recorded and studied by delicate mechanisms, to be translated, perhaps, into warnings of future volcanic eruptions or disastrous earthquakes.

Cosmic rays and radio waves are bounced back from the sky. Nuclear research programs study the awesome energy within the atom. Here is potential power for industry, transportation and daily life.

Planes and missiles are designed and tested on offshore islands.

Scientists are continually finding and testing new uses for old materials. They search for new products to meet new needs. They search for ways man can better use his knowledge, his skills and the bounty of his environment. The profits of this modern treasure hunt in the lands of the Pacific are not only for the people of this region but will benefit our entire country and our world in man's desire for a good today and mankind's search for a better tomorrow.

Things to think about

How has man used the vast natural wealth of the Pacific States?

How do the rivers and the great valleys affect the ways people live in the Pacific States?

Consider the relationship between the land and the way the people live in our two newest states, Alaska and Hawaii.

In what ways have foreign words and customs become a part of our American tradition?

Enchanting lands of the Pacific

There is enchantment in the islands, the polar peninsula, and the rugged coastlands of the Pacific States. There is natural beauty and grandeur in a vast kaleidoscope of climates, land forms and colors. Fascination waits in wonderland varieties of plants and animals.

Explore and Enjoy

Many of the most interesting sights to see and things to do are found near the ocean and on the lakes and streams. Try beach combing, kayak or hydroplane races, ferryboat rides, log-rolling contests, surf-casting or deep-sea fishing. Ride a rushing wave on a surfboard or in an outrigger canoe in the wonderland waters of the Pacific States.

You can watch the *Blessing of the Fleet* at the opening of the halibut season in Petersburg, Alaska, or see the waves carry out thousands of flower wreaths from all over the world at the memorial service of the *Fleet of Flowers* at Depoe Bay, Oregon. You can see shrimp peeling and crab shaking contests in Kodiak. You can admire the giant, finny winners of the salmon derbies.

A simple walk along a fishermen's wharf can be as exciting as watching freighters and ocean liners from all over the world being eased into their berths in ocean ports.

The patchwork of climates and natural regions of the Pacific States provides activities and sights that are poles apart.

Exciting dog-sled-races and baseball games on snowshoes, or played under the midnight sun, can be seen in Alaska.

Cattle drives, roundups and fast-paced rodeos are part of the Washington and Oregon scene.

Snowy, breath-taking toboggan slides and ski runs are just a few miles from the glass-bottomed boats that let you see the wonders of the ocean floor near Santa Catalina Island, California.

Oriental bazaars, torchlight fishing, Polynesian luaus, water buffalo wading in rice paddies are all part of Hawaii. Here, too, you can see the only king's palace in America. Iolani Palace is now the Hawaiian state capitol building.

In Hollywood, you may see a Roman Emperor's palace on a movie set.

You can walk into Frontierland, Fantasyland, and Tomorrowland at Disneyland.

You can trace footprints, handprints and autographs of movie stars in the cement at Graumann's Chinese Theater.

You can see the skeletons of prehistoric animals at the treacherous La Brea tar pits where they were trapped long ago.

There are Spanish fiestas, Indian tribal ceremonials, Eskimo dances, winter carnivals and strawberry festivals. There are Gold Rush Days, Russian Christmas and Chinese New Year celebrations. Take your pick. Enchantment waits in the lands of the Pacific.

High and Low Lands and Lakes

The scenery of the Pacific States is a spectacular mosaic of colors and forms. Snow-frosted mountain ranges glitter in the sun, their lofty peaks lost in the clouds. Ice cliffs and deep crevasses hold fascination and danger. Thousands of lakes mirror the sky. Foaming falls plunge from high cliffs into cool, green glades. Shifting sand dunes tower along the coastal beaches where white-tipped breakers crash. The tides whisper in and out of gentle coves.

The desert areas have color and grandeur of their own, and mystical mirages.

58

Gorges and canyons, cut by rivers, are tinted in paintbox colors.

Under the earth, eerie blue light radiates from fantastic formations in ice caves. Grand pillars of marble, water-carved from the earth's interior through the ages, gleam in the splendor of underground caverns.

Black sand beaches and lava flow lands of twisted beauty are the volcanic inheritance of the land.

Towering redwoods and sequoias lift their trunks hundreds of feet into the sky. Some of them have looked down upon thousands of years of history.

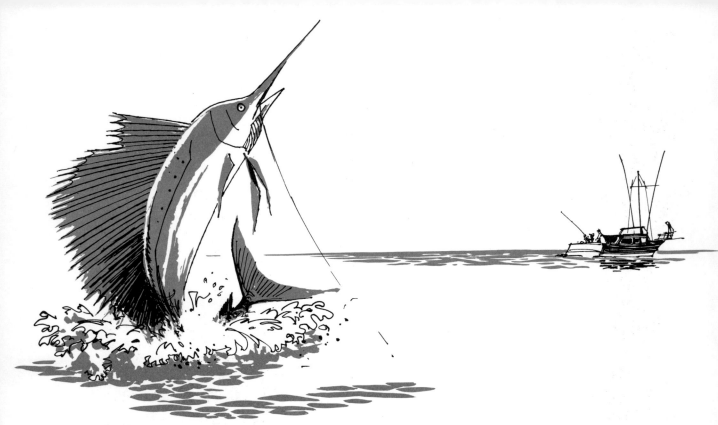

Wildlife of the Pacific Lands and Waters

There is a wide variety of wildlife—animal, fish and fowl—in the Pacific States to delight any hunter, fisherman, naturalist or camera bug.

Dolphin, marlin, sailfish, swordfish and tuna challenge the deep-sea fisherman's skill and endurance. Strange little fish with an odd-sounding name, *wahoo*, drift in the warm ocean currents.

Some fishermen go after the giant King salmon and spunky trout for sport and food.

Clams and mussels can be dug along the beaches. At dawn or dusk along Puget Sound, there is real sport in trying to out-dig the delicious but evasive gooey-duck clams coming out of the mud at low tide. Wild ducks, geese and other waterfowl fly high over land and lakes on their way to and from summer homes in the far north. Nesting sea birds colonize the offshore rocks. Ptarmigan, grouse and pheasant scurry through brush. Tiny, rainbow-hued birds, the *apapane*, and *amakihi*, add to the brilliance of jungle flowers.

The mighty polar bear is at home on the arctic ice floes. The poor musk ox is getting a second chance in Alaska. Because of his utter fearlessness, he was all but wiped out when hunters came to the land.

Giant bears, moose, caribou, all sorts of deer, mountain sheep and goats, elk and bison roam the mountains.

Smaller, but far from harmless, are the predators—the coyotes, bobcats and mountain lions of the rocky hillsides and ravines.

There are no rabbits or squirrels in Hawaii. Daring sportsmen pick wild pigs for dangerous island opponents.

If it is fur you are after, mink, fox, muskrat, beaver, martin, lynx and ermine can be found in the northlands. But remember that Indians, Eskimos and Aleuts hunt them for a living and the supply is dwindling.

Fish and wildlife services and game commissions have been set up to protect animals and birds that are in danger of extinction from greed and carelessness. Wildlife is a great natural resource that must be used wisely. Now, fish hatcheries, game farms, wildlife preserves and refuges, restricted hunting areas and seasons help to assure a continuing supply and wise use of our wildlife resources.

National Parks and Monuments of The Pacific States

Within the far-flung wonderland of the Pacific States there are many areas with special natural charm and unique features preserved by the National Park Service so that we may enjoy and learn from them the wonders of our land, its wildlife and its history.

Caves, Canyons, Forests

Oregon Caves National Monument gives the visitor a glimpse of nature's wonderful way with water and land. Oregon's marble cavern, carved out over the centuries by running waters, contains water-sculptured formations of great variety and beauty.

Kings Canyon National Park in California is set in the wilderness of the Sierra Nevadas, dominated by two enormous canyons cut out by the Kings River. Here you can read chapters from the story of the land in formations written by upheavals of the earth and the action of the elements.

Yosemite National Park in California also affords a picturesque example of results crafted by natural forces. The great U-shaped valley of the park was chiseled and ground out by slow-moving glaciers. The ice-age glaciers cut sheer granite cliffs and deep gorges from which roaring waterfalls now tumble on their way to the rivers below. Both Yosemite and Kings Canyon count groves of giant sequoias among their spectacular features.

Muir Woods National Monument, California, has perhaps the most inspiring stand of redwoods reaching skyward.

Sequoia National Park, California, has great groves of forest giants, the sequoias, that are among the world's largest and oldest living things. These towering monarchs cling to life even when they have been uprooted. New shoots branch off from the trunks of fallen trees and develop into new giants, each with its own root system. Sequoia National Park, set in magnificent High Sierra scenery, includes the lofty snow-capped peak of Mount Whitney.

Olympic National Park in Washington, contains the finest remnants of the Pacific Northwest rain forests, made lush by the rains of centuries. Here, too, are unspoiled mountain wilderness and active glaciers.

63

Ancient Ice Memorials

Mount Rainier National Park, Washington; Mount McKinley National Park, Alaska; and Glacier Bay National Monument, Alaska; are tributes to ice-clad mountain magnificence.

For tens of thousands of years, glaciers have carved out the land. Within Mount McKinley National Park, jagged spires, sharp ridges and broad, U-shaped valleys are sculptured evidence of the Ice Age. Mount McKinley, North America's highest peak, towers above 3,000 square miles of wilderness.

Great, active tidewater glaciers form high, ice-topped mountains in Alaska's Glacier Bay National Monument. Here you can see interglacial and various stages of post-glacial forests and rare species of wildlife.

Glaciers radiate from the summit and slopes of the defunct volcano, Mount Rainier. Forest wilderness and blooming meadows flank its sides.

Monuments of Volcanic Violence

Alaska's Katmai National Monument is an active volcanic region. Here is the Valley of Ten Thousand Smokes which was the scene of violent eruptions at the turn of the century. Now Mount Trident and Mount Novarupta look down on the last of the valley's dwindling steam spouts. Katmai National Monument is the home of the brown bear, the world's largest carnivore.

Lassen Volcanic National Park in California was last active in the early 1900's. Here is an area of hot springs, cinder cones, lava flows and lakes.

Lava Beds National Monument, California, exhibits recent lava flows and lava caves.

Crater Lake National Park in Oregon, is an example of beauty and splendor created by volcanic violence. The deep, blue lake in the old crater of the shattered Mount Mazama is of exceptional beauty, set in a landscape of forested slopes and towering, snow-capped peaks.

Pinnacles National Monument, California, encloses spire-like rock formations of towering heights with many caves and a variety of volcanic features.

Devils Postpile National Monument in California, is made up of towering formations of blue-gray basaltic columns that fit together like the pipes of a mammoth organ.

In Hawaii National Park the volcanoes Kilauea and Mauna Loa slope toward each other, intertwined by centuries of lava flows. Within the great crater depressions of Kilauea is a boiling lake of lava which sometimes rises and overflows onto the crater floor. At other times, the boiling lake sinks from sight. Violent steam explosions follow the sinking. Late in the 1700's one of these violent steam explosions, accompanied by hot blasts of rock and dust, overtook and killed part of a native army on the march. Prints of bare feet were preserved in layers of wet volcanic ash and may be seen in the desert, miles from the crater. Since then, other eruptions have broken through the crater walls forming lava lakes as much as sixty-three feet deep.

Lava flows from the giant Mauna Loa cover more than 2,000 square miles. Since man has watched this fiery mountain it has been alternately quiet and violently active. A series of earthquakes and molten rock forcing its way through cracks to the surface warn of eruptions and lava flows to come.

Haleakala, on the island of Maui, is an old volcano in the last stages of life. Its eruptions may be hundreds of years apart. Haleakala means "House of the Sun." In legend, Maui, a Polynesian demi-god climbed to the top of the volcano, ensnared the sun and forced it to travel more slowly to give his mother enough hours of sunlight to finish her work. The Haleakala region became a separate national park on July 1, 1961.

Luxuriant tropical forests, colorful native birds, spectacular cliffs and rugged coastlines, barren lava flows and moving dunes of desert lands add wonder and beauty to these volcanic monuments.

Desert Monuments

Death Valley National Monument is shared by California and Nevada. It became famous in the history of the west and in the tales of gold rush days. Here is a vast desert solitude with weird, natural formations of glittering borax and extensive salt beds. Within the monument is the lowest point in the Western Hemisphere, 282 feet below sea level.

Joshua Tree National Monument in California, is a splendid vista of desert country. Here, magnificent stands of Joshua trees, cholla cactus and other desert plants are preserved in a striking setting of granite formations.

Island Sanctuary

Channel Islands National Monument includes the Santa Barbara and Anacapa Islands of California. A large rookery of sea lions, many nesting birds and unusual plants make these islands interesting.

Landmarks of Yesterday

Fort Clatsop National Monument, Oregon, where Lewis and Clark spent the winter of 1805-1806 preparing for their long return journey to St. Louis, has been reconstructed for us to see today.

Fort Vancouver National Monument, Washington, was the western headquarters of the Hudson's Bay Company and the military and trading hub of the Northwest for a hundred years.

Whitman National Monument, Washington, marks the place on the Oregon Trail where the pioneer missionaries, Dr. Marcus Whitman and his wife, ministered to the Indians.

Sitka National Monument, Alaska, is the site of the Indian stockade where Indians made their last stand against the Russian settlers. There is a fine exhibit of old totem poles collected from many places.

Cabrillo National Monument commemorates Cabrillo's discovery of San Diego Bay in 1542. Cabrillo's find was the first European contact with that part of the world.

City of Refuge National Historical Park, Hawaii, is considered to be the most impressive monument to ancient Hawaii. It was a place of sacred refuge enclosed by a great stone wall where, hundreds of years ago, criminals could find haven.

Things to think about

What is there in the Pacific States to attract a hunter . . . a fisherman . . . a geologist . . . a camera bug?

Why have some areas of the Pacific States been set aside as national parks and monuments?

What are ways in which wildlife is protected from greed and misuse?

What are some of the things that make the Pacific States especially enchanting in their recreational opportunities and scenic beauty?

69

ALASKA
Capital: Juneau
Area: 586,400 square miles Rank: 1st
Population: 226,167 Rank: 50th
Admission Date: January 3, 1959
Rank: 49th

Major Sources of Income:
Fisheries
salmon, halibut, herring, cod, shell-fish
Forestry
hemlock, spruce, cedar, birch
Minerals
coal, gold, platinum, lead, silver, copper

Climate:
Alaska is not a frozen wasteland. Along the Pacific Coast, the climate is mild and wet. Sometimes as much as 230 inches of rain fall in one year. Winters may be stormy but are not exceptionally cold; summers are cool with plenty of rain and fog. Interior Alaska has very light rainfall and great extremes of temperature. Arctic Alaska is cool, 40 degrees in July; 19 below zero in January; and dry, averaging only 5 inches of rain or snow each year.

William H. Seward American states-man responsible for the far-sighted purchase of Alaska in 1867

Jack London American sailor and Klondike gold-seeker who wrote adventurous tales of Alaska

State Flower: Forget-me-not

State Flag

State Seal

State Bird: Ptarmigan

Arctic Ocean
Barrow   Pt. Barrow
Beaufort Sea
CANADA

U.S.S.R.
International Date Line
Chukchi Sea
Colville River
BROOKS RANGE
ARCTIC
Noatak River
Baird Mts.
Kotzebue
CIRCLE
Monday
Sunday
Bering Strait
Seward Peninsula
College
Fairbanks
St. Lawrence Island
Nome
Norton Sound
Yukon River
Tanana River
Kuskokwim Mts.
Mt. McKinley
RANGE
Kuskokwim River
Mt. McKinley Nat'l. Park
Wrangell Mts.
Cape Romanzof
ALASKA
Palmer
Bethel
Anchorage
Mt. St. Elias
Cordova
Nunivak Island
Prince William Sound
Skagway
CANADA
Bering
Iliamna Lake
Cook Inlet
Seward
Glacier Bay Nat'l. Mon.
JUNEAU
Pribilof Islands
Katmai Nat'l. Mon.
Douglas
Sea
Bristol Bay
Gulf of Alaska
ALEXANDER
Sitka
Petersburg
Wrangell
Kodiak Island
Sitka Nat'l. Mon.
Islands of the Four Mts.
Kodiak
Pacific   Ocean
Ketchikan
Alaska Peninsula
Aleutian Range
ARCHIPELAGO
ALEUTIAN ISLANDS
Near Islands
ALEUTIAN ISLANDS
Islands of the Four Mts.
Rat Islands
Andreanof Islands

Even though the great land mass of Alaska was purchased from Russia almost one hundred years ago, it is our second newest state. It is also our largest state, one-fifth the size of the continental United States and two and one-half times the size of Texas.

The length of Alaska's rugged coastline exceeds the length of all the other coasts of the United States combined.

Important Whens and Whats in the Making of Alaska

1728   Vitus Bering finds that the polar peninsula is part of the North American continent.

1741   Russian explorers discover Alaska.

1778   Captain Cook makes extensive surveys for the British Government.

1784   Russians make the first settlement at Three Saints on Kodiak Island.

1806   The capital is moved from Kodiak to Sitka.

1867   The United States purchases Alaska from Russia.

1884   Alaska becomes a United States Territory.

1897   The gold rush in the Klondike brings many people to the north lands.

1958   Alaska is admitted to the Union as the 49th state.

Three distinct regions make up Alaska, our new frontier.

The Pacific Region's great length is bordered by the Coast Ranges. These Pacific mountains contain vast mineral resources, including copper, gold, silver, and other ores. Coal fields lie further inland.

Pacific Alaska leads the world in the catching and canning of salmon.

The Central Region of Alaska is separated from the Pacific Region by the great Alaska Range. The hilly, plateau country of Central Alaska is drained by the mighty Yukon River and its branches the Tanana and Koyukuk.

There are fertile farmlands in the central valleys. The Matanuska and Tanana Valleys are Alaska's farming centers. Hardy vegetables, small fruits, berries, and some grains are grown. Dairy cattle and some sheep and hogs are raised.

Arctic Alaska includes the treeless coastal plain, the tundra, beyond the boundaries of the Arctic Circle. The only inhabitants of this region are the Eskimo families that live near Point Barrow. Reindeer, the semi-domesticated relatives of the caribou, brought from Siberia, provide the Eskimos with food, and hides for clothing and tents.

Lumber, shingles, fuel, pulp and other forest products come from southeastern Alaska's stands of spruce, hemlock, cedar and birch.

Fur farms raise minks and foxes to supplement Alaska's natural fur resources. Some pelts are taken from the fur seals of the Pribilof Islands.

Alaska can be reached by steamships from Seattle that travel the inside passage between the islands and the coastland, by the great Alaska Highway that stretches to Fairbanks, or by airplane.

Less than one hundred years ago, this vast land became a possession of the United States for the sum of $7,200,000. Since then, three times that sum is made yearly from Alaska's minerals. A great new frontier and a wonderful future wait in Alaska.

OREGON

NEVADA

CALIFORNIA
Area: 158,693 square miles
Population: 15,717,204
Admission Date: September 9, 1850

Capital: Sacramento
Rank: 3rd
Rank: 2nd
Rank: 31st

Major Sources of Income:

Manufacturing and Processing
aircraft, food products, electrical equipment, chemicals

Agriculture and Livestock
beef cattle and dairy products, field crops, fruit and nuts

Minerals
petroleum and natural gas, stone, clay and glass

Climate:
Rainfall is a vital factor in California's climate. Annual rainfall varies from over 100 inches in the northwest to 2 inches or less in the southwest. California's climate ranges from frostless belts of warmth where subtropical fruits and flowers thrive to the arctic zones of ice-capped mountain peaks. Along the seacoast and the interior valleys where most of the people live, California has the usual climate of two seasons. In the winter months it rains, but there is no snow since temperatures seldom drop below freezing. The summer and fall are dry. Along the coast, ocean fogs and breezes modify the dry summer heat and nights are cool.

Lava Beds Nat'l. Mon.
Mt. Shasta
Cascade Range
Shasta Dam
Lassen Peak
Lassen Volcanic Nat'l. Park

Humboldt Bay

Pacific Ocean

SIERRA
Sacramento Valley
Sacramento River
Squaw Valley
Lake Tahoe
Coloma
SACRAMENTO
Sonoma
Stockton
Berkeley
Oakland
San Francisco
Palo Alto
San Jose
San Joaquin River
San Joaquin Valley
NEVADA

Yosemite Nat'l. Park
Devils Postpile Nat'l. Mon.
Kings Canyon Nat'l. Park
Sequoia Nat'l. Park
Mt. Whitney

Monterey Bay
Pinnacles Nat'l. Mon.
COAST
Salinas
Monterey
RANGES
Fresno

Death Valley Nat'l. Mon.

State Flower:
Golden Poppy

State Bird:
Valley Quail

CALIFORNIA REPUBLIC

State Flag

THE GREAT SEAL OF THE STATE OF CALIFORNIA

State Seal

Pacific Ocean

Bakersfield
San Luis Obispo
Burbank
Mt. Wilson
Glendale
Pasadena
San Bernardino
Santa Barbara
Beverly Hills
Los Angeles
Riverside
San Miguel Island
Santa Cruz Island
Long Beach
Palm Springs
Santa Ana
Palomar Mtn.
Palomar Observatory
Salton Sea

MOJAVE DESERT
Joshua Tree Nat'l. Mon.
Colorado River

El Cajon Imperial Valley
San Diego
Chula Vista

Santa Catalina Island
Channel Islands Nat'l. Mon.
San Clemente Island

MEXICO

Luther Burbank
American plant breeder

Leland Stanford
Founded Stanford University

John C. Frémont
One of the first American explorers in California

Herbert Hoover
31st President of the U.S.

FAMOUS CALIFORNIANS

Mountain highlands, desert drylands, fertile farmlands are all part of California, our third largest state.

California is ringed by mountains. The Coast Ranges rise above the Pacific. The Sacramento and San Joaquin Rivers join to break through these barriers and flow to the ocean. The snow-peaked Sierra Nevadas rise on California's eastern boundary. Mountains mark the northlands and scattered ranges dot the southern sections. Highlands surround California's Central Valley, made fertile by streams born in the high Sierras.

Important Whens and Whats in the Making of California

1540 Hernando de Alarcón is the first white man to set foot within California's present borders.

1579 England's Sir Francis Drake beaches the *Golden Hind* near what is now San Francisco and claims the territory for Queen Elizabeth.

1769 Four expeditions from Mexico head for California and Father Junípero Serra builds the first mission settlement at San Diego.

1822 Mexico gains independence from Spain and the California region comes under the flag of Mexico.

1846 The Bear Flag revolt by American settlers against Mexico sets up the California Republic.

1848 Mexico gives up California to the United States by the Treaty of Guadalupe Hidalgo.
Gold is discovered in the tail race of John Sutter's lumber mill at Coloma.

1850 California is admitted to the Union as the 31st state.

Desert lands and the great Imperial Valley, where crops grow the year around, lie in the southeast. Orange and lemon groves bask in the warmth of the San Bernardino Valley that stretches westward to the sea.

Blessed by long growing seasons, California is a leading agricultural state. Even in southern California, the most thickly populated region, there are many small farms.

The Central Valley boasts of farms of a thousand acres or more in size. This section is the vineyard of California. Here, too, many fields of flowers grown for seeds and bulbs color the land. Cattle and sheep are raised in the highlands that ring the Central Valley.

Vegetables, berries, cantaloupes, grapes, olives, figs, dates and cotton come from the Imperial Valley, irrigated by the Colorado River.

From the deep mountain forests come redwood, spruce and pine for lumber and many other wood products. About one-half of California's forest land is government controlled.

California's towering high spot, Mount Whitney, contrasts sharply with the Death Valley lowpoint that lies more than two hundred feet below sea level.

California's desolate Mojave Desert suppies the world with borax.

Oil, the result of processes begun in the time when dinosaurs walked the land, lies under the ocean floor in off-shore oil fields and beneath southern California's oil-rich earth.

Seaside San Diego is California's fishing center, and the location of one of our country's big naval bases. Here is Mission San Diego de Alcala, the first of the California missions built by Father Junípero Serra. Here is San Diego Bay discovered two hundred years before by Juan Rodrigues Cabrillo.

Fresno, in the Central Valley, is the center of the grape industry.

Los Angeles makes airplanes, tires, furniture, clothing, and films for movies and television. Los Angeles refines oil and natural gas for commercial and industrial use.

San Francisco, home of the great Golden Gate Bridge, is a busy seaport center of commerce, decked out with sidewalk flower stands and the colorful quarter of Chinatown.

California is the old land of ancient sequoias, lofty mountains and tumbling waterfalls; of Spanish towns and missions, and the gold rush. California is the new land of oil and industry, fruit and fish, movies and television.

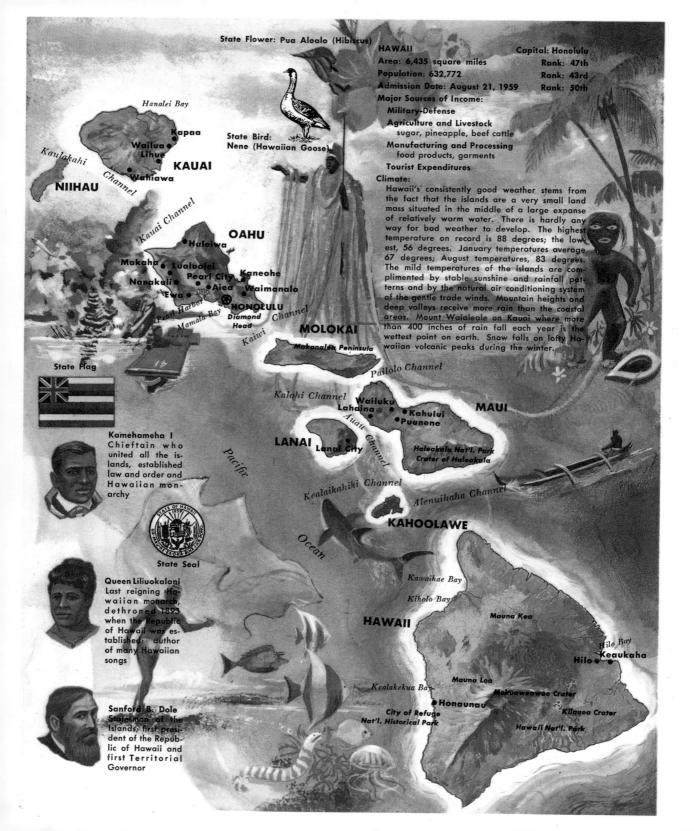

State Flower: Pua Aloalo (Hibiscus)

HAWAII
Area: 6,435 square miles
Population: 632,772
Admission Date: August 21, 1959

Capital: Honolulu
Rank: 47th
Rank: 43rd
Rank: 50th

Major Sources of Income:

Military-Defense

Agriculture and Livestock
sugar, pineapple, beef cattle

Manufacturing and Processing
food products, garments

Tourist Expenditures

Climate:

Hawaii's consistently good weather stems from the fact that the islands are a very small land mass situated in the middle of a large expanse of relatively warm water. There is hardly any way for bad weather to develop. The highest temperature on record is 88 degrees; the lowest, 56 degrees. January temperatures average 67 degrees; August temperatures, 83 degrees. The mild temperatures of the islands are complimented by stable sunshine and rainfall patterns and by the natural air conditioning system of the gentle trade winds. Mountain heights and deep valleys receive more rain than the coastal areas. Mount Waialeale on Kauai where more than 400 inches of rain fall each year is the wettest point on earth. Snow falls on lofty Hawaiian volcanic peaks during the winter.

State Bird: Nene (Hawaiian Goose)

Hanalei Bay
Kapaa
Wailua
Lihue
KAUAI
Wahiawa

Kaulakahi Channel

NIIHAU

Kauai Channel

OAHU
Haleiwa
Makaha
Lualualei
Pearl City
Kaneohe
Nanakuli
Aiea
Waimanalo
Ewa
HONOLULU
Pearl Harbor
Diamond Head
Mamala Bay
Kaiwi Channel

State Flag

Kamehameha I Chieftain who united all the islands, established law and order and Hawaiian monarchy

State Seal

Queen Liliuokalani Last reigning Hawaiian monarch, dethroned 1893 when the Republic of Hawaii was established; author of many Hawaiian songs

Sanford B. Dole Statesman of the Islands; first president of the Republic of Hawaii and first Territorial Governor

MOLOKAI
Makanalua Peninsula

Pailolo Channel

Kalohi Channel
Wailuku
Lahaina
Kahului
Puunene
MAUI
Auau Channel

LANAI
Lanai City
Haleakala Nat'l. Park
Crater of Haleakala

Kealaikahiki Channel

Alenuihaha Channel

KAHOOLAWE

Pacific

Ocean

Kawaihae Bay
Kiholo Bay
Mauna Kea

HAWAII
Kealakekua Bay
Mauna Loa
Hilo Bay
Keaukaha
Hilo
Mokuaweoweo Crater
Honaunau
Kilauea Crater
City of Refuge Nat'l. Historical Park
Hawaii Nat'l. Park

Hawaii, our fiftieth state, is made up of a chain of many reefs, shoals and islands that reaches 1,500 miles out over the central Pacific. Over millions of years this chain of underwater mountains, the longest in the world, was built up from the ocean floor by out-pouring lava.

Hawaii is known to the world for her eight main islands, a total area less than that of New Jersey, but greater than Delaware, Connecticut, or Rhode Island. In order of size, the main Hawaiian Islands are Hawaii, Maui, Oahu, where more than 78 per cent of the people live, Kauai, Molokai, Lanai, Niihau, and Kahoolawe.

Important Whens and Whats in the Making of Hawaii

1778 England's James Cook, captain of an exploratory fleet, sails into Waimea Bay, Kaui Island.

1795 Kamehameha, Hawaii Island chief, unites islands after defeating other island chiefs.

1820 Missionaries arrive from New England.

1850 Kamehameha III declares Honolulu the capital city.

1852 The first Chinese arrive in Hawaii; Japanese, Portuguese, Spanish, Filipinos follow.

1893 Queen Liliuokalani is dethroned. The Republic of Hawaii is created.

1898 Hawaii becomes a United States Territory.

1927 The first successful non-stop flight is made from California to Hawaii.

1941 Japan attacks Pearl Harbor, marking the entry of the United States into World War II.

1959 Hawaii is admitted to the Union as the 50th state.

Bordered by the Pacific on every side and punctuated with mountain peaks that reach toward 14,000 feet above the sea, Hawaii contains some of the most beautiful scenery in the world. Mark Twain called Hawaii "the most beautiful fleet of islands anchored in any ocean."

Hawaii's ever-green landscape is etched with floral colors and surrounded by sparkling sea. The gentle, spring-like climate and the rich, lava soil provide an ideal year-round growing season. Sugar cane is grown on irrigated lowland plantations. Pineapples flourish in drier soils. Pineapple is the only crop on the island of Lanai where more than 200,000 tons are produced each year.

Fields of tiny, lavender Vanda orchids tint the landscape. Small farms yield coffee, tropical fruits, rice, potatoes and onions. Large ranches supply sheep and cattle to the islands and the mainland. Fishing fleets ring the coastlines and bays.

The conversion of cane into sugar and the canning of pineapple, the manufacturing and processing of other products are part of Hawaii's industrial scheme.

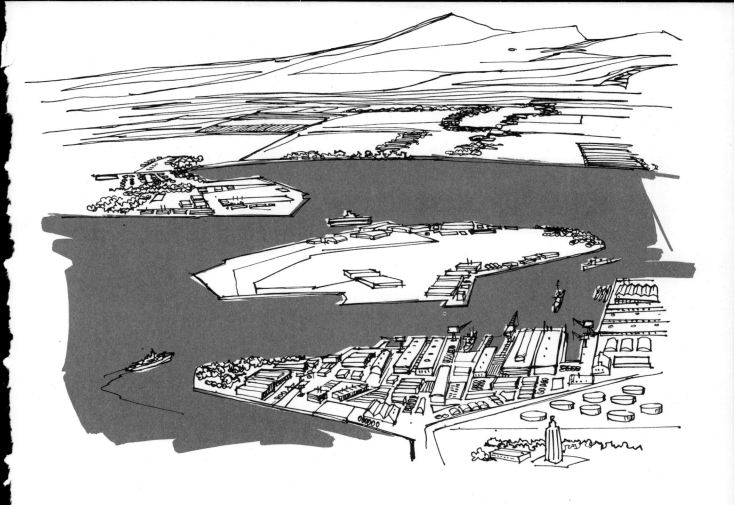

Military and defense installations and operations play a great part in Hawaii's economy. The natural harbor of Pearl Harbor on Oahu furnishes our navy with an important base.

Oahu's Honolulu, (*hono*—a valley with a bay; *lulu*—sheltered;) is the main city of the islands. It has been the capital city since 1850 when King Kamehameha III made it his permanent residence. Here is the capitol building, Iolani Palace, where the state flag, designed before 1816 for King Kamehameha I, flies beside the Stars and Stripes.

Hawaii, geographically, is the crossroads of the Pacific. In her ports lie ships of many nations.

Visitors come from everywhere to enjoy Hawaii's climate and the scenic beauty of volcanoes and snowfields, lush jungles and pounding surf, and the pageantry of Hawaiian history and customs.

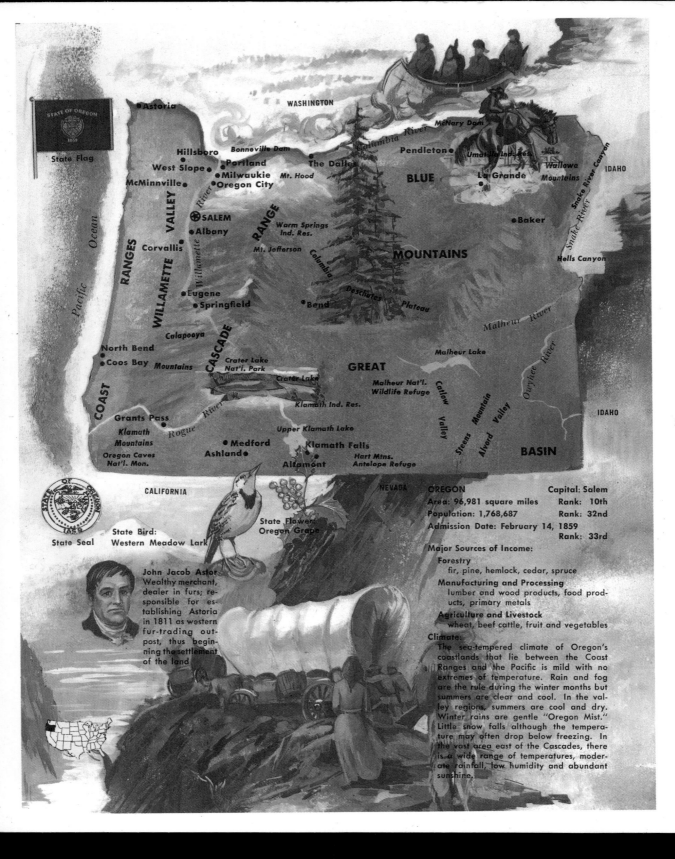

WASHINGTON

Astoria

State Flag

Hillsboro
West Slope
Portland
Milwaukie
McMinnville
Oregon City

Bonneville Dam
The Dalles
Mt. Hood

Columbia River

McNary Dam
Pendleton
Umatilla Ind. Res.
La Grande

BLUE

Wallowa
Mountains

IDAHO

WILLAMETTE VALLEY

Willamette River

SALEM
Albany
Corvallis

Warm Springs
Ind. Res.
Mt. Jefferson

RANGE

Columbia

MOUNTAINS

Baker

Snake River

Snake River Canyon

Hells Canyon

COAST RANGES

Pacific Ocean

Eugene
Springfield

Calapooya

North Bend
Coos Bay

CASCADE Mountains

Bend

Deschutes Plateau

Malheur River

Crater Lake
Nat'l. Park

Crater Lake

GREAT

Malheur Lake

Malheur Nat'l.
Wildlife Refuge

Ouyhee River

IDAHO

Grants Pass

Klamath
Mountains

Rogue River

Klamath Ind. Res.

Upper Klamath Lake

Catlow Valley

Steens Mountain

Alvord Valley

Oregon Caves
Nat'l. Mon.

Medford
Ashland

Klamath Falls

Altamont

Hart Mtns.
Antelope Refuge

BASIN

State Seal

CALIFORNIA

NEVADA

State Bird:
Western Meadow Lark

State Flower:
Oregon Grape

John Jacob Astor
Wealthy merchant,
dealer in furs; re-
sponsible for es-
tablishing Astoria
in 1811 as western
fur-trading out-
post, thus begin-
ning the settlement
of the land

OREGON
Area: 96,981 square miles
Population: 1,768,687
Admission Date: February 14, 1859

Capital: Salem
Rank: 10th
Rank: 32nd
Rank: 33rd

Major Sources of Income:

Forestry
fir, pine, hemlock, cedar, spruce

Manufacturing and Processing
lumber and wood products, food products, primary metals

Agriculture and Livestock
wheat, beef cattle, fruit and vegetables

Climate:
The sea-tempered climate of Oregon's
coastlands that lie between the Coast
Ranges and the Pacific is mild with no
extremes of temperature. Rain and fog
are the rule during the winter months but
summers are clear and cool. In the valley regions, summers are cool and dry.
Winter rains are gentle "Oregon Mist."
Little snow falls although the temperature may often drop below freezing. In
the vast area east of the Cascades, there
is a wide range of temperatures, moderate rainfall, low humidity and abundant
sunshine.

The area that we now call Oregon was once the southern section of the great territory, Oregon Country, that extended from California all the way to Alaska. The southern portion was soon known for its fur-bearing animals and many beaver colonies and attracted early trappers and traders.

The rugged north-south ranges of the Cascades divide present-day Oregon into two main regions.

Western Oregon is the land of the Willamette Valley and low Coast Ranges, fertile valleys and vast forests.

Important Whens and Whats in the Making of Oregon

1543 Spanish seamen voyage up the coast from Mexico.

1788 Captain Robert Gray, sailing along the extent of Oregon's coastline is the first white man known to set foot on Oregon soil.

1791-92 Captain Gray discovers the Columbia River, sails upstream, gives it the name of his ship and establishes a claim for the United States.

1793 Alexander Mackenzie makes the first successful overland expedition to the Pacific Coast from Canada.

1805 Lewis and Clark reach the Pacific's shores after their overland journey from St. Louis.

1811 Astoria is built by the Pacific Fur Company.

1848 Oregon Territory is created.

1853 Washington Territory is cut away from Oregon.

1859 Oregon is admitted to the Union as the 33rd state.

83

East of the Cascades is the far larger region of high, arid plateaus, small rich river valleys, towering Mount Hood and the violently born beauty of Crater Lake.

The rich soil, plentiful rainfall and mild climate of the Willamette Valley make this region Oregon's farmland. Dairy farms, farms that produce fruits and berries, and rainbow fields of flowers grown for seed bloom in the rich river valley. Hogs, sheep and cattle thrive high above the valley on dry grass-land plateaus.

The rains are held in the valley by the barrier of the Cascades. On the eastern, drier side of the Cascades, dry farming produces grains. A dam across the Owyhee River stores water for irrigation.

From the vast forest lands come Douglas fir, redwood, spruce and hardwoods. Lumbering is Oregon's most important industry.

Fishing fleets sail the ocean, rivers, and streams to bring in salmon for Oregon's canneries.

Power is generated from Oregon's rushing rivers and streams. The great Bonneville Dam on the Columbia River supplies power and light for thousands of homes and industries.

Spain, England and Russia originally claimed the Oregon Country. The United States' claim and ultimate possession was based on the early voyages of Captain Gray and the history-making overland trip of Lewis and Clark. The first settlement in Oregon was made by an American fur company. Since then the face of the land has changed. From the wilderness rose great cities.

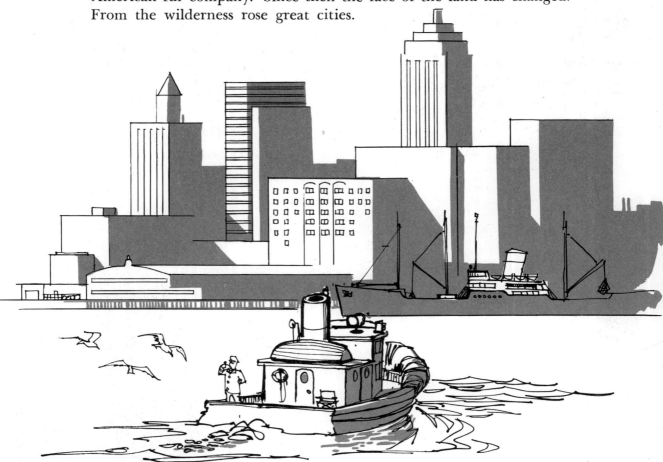

Portland is a busy ocean-river port, a great trade and manufacturing center. Astoria, no longer John Jacob Astor's great western fur post, is now the hub of Oregon's fish-packing activities. Industry and agriculture center in Salem and Eugene.

Timbered mountain, rich river valley, high plateau, busy port, fertile farmland and lumber mill are the face of Oregon today.

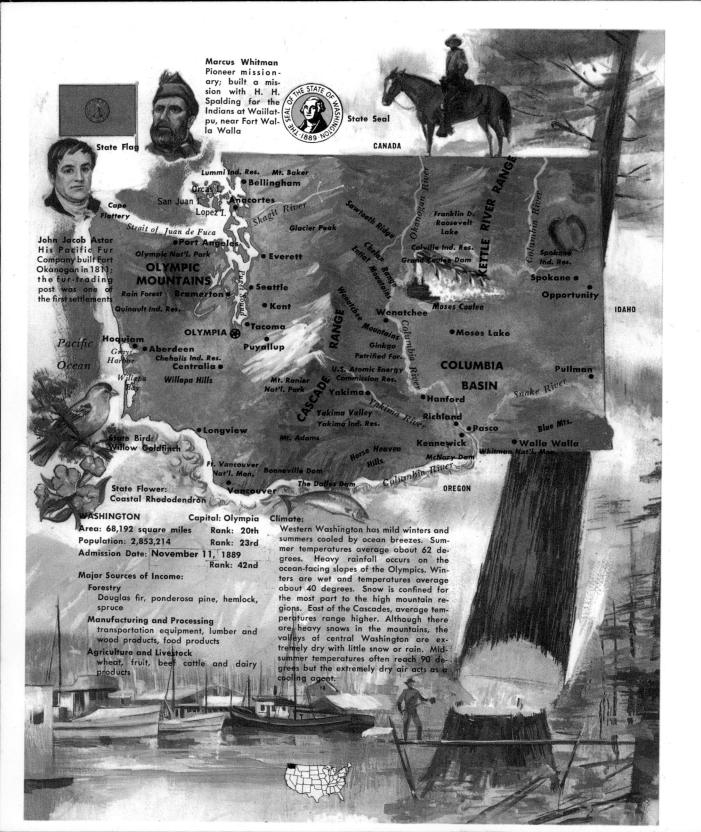

State Flag

Marcus Whitman Pioneer missionary; built a mission with H. H. Spalding for the Indians at Waiilatpu, near Fort Walla Walla

THE SEAL OF THE STATE OF WASHINGTON · 1889 · **State Seal**

CANADA

John Jacob Astor His Pacific Fur Company built Fort Okanogan in 1811; the fur-trading post was one of the first settlements

Lummi Ind. Res.   Mt. Baker
Orcas I.   ● Bellingham
San Juan I. ● Anacortes
Lopez I.
Cape
Flattery   Skagit River
Strait of Juan de Fuca   Glacier Peak
Port Angeles
Olympic Nat'l. Park
OLYMPIC   ● Everett
MOUNTAINS
Rain Forest   ● Bremerton   ● Seattle
Quinault Ind. Res.
                    ● Kent
                  ● Tacoma
Pacific   Hoquiam   OLYMPIA ⊛
         ● Aberdeen   ● Puyallup
Ocean   Grays
         Harbor   Chehalis Ind. Res.
               Centralia ●
         Willapa   Willapa Hills
         Bay

Sawtooth Ridge
Chelan
Range   Okanogan River   Franklin D.
Entiat   Roosevelt
Mountains   Lake   Columbia River
                Colville Ind. Res.   KETTLE RIVER RANGE
         Grand Coulee Dam   Spokane
RANGE   ● Wenatchee   Ind. Res.
Wenatchee   Moses Coulee   ● Spokane
Mountains   Columbia River   ● Opportunity
         Ginkgo   ● Moses Lake
         Petrified For.   IDAHO
CASCADE U.S. Atomic Energy   **COLUMBIA**
         Commission Res.   **BASIN**   ● Pullman
Mt. Ranier   ● Hanford   Snake River
Nat'l. Park   ● Yakima
         Yakima Valley   Yakima River ● Richland   Blue Mts.
         Yakima Ind. Res.   ● Pasco
● Longview   ● Walla Walla
         Mt. Adams   Horse Heaven   Kennewick
                    Hills   McNary Dam   Whitman Nat'l. Mon.
State Bird: Ft. Vancouver
Willow Goldfinch   Nat'l. Mon.   Bonneville Dam
                The Dalles Dam   Columbia River
State Flower: ● Vancouver   OREGON
Coastal Rhododendron

WASHINGTON   Capital: Olympia

Area: 68,192 square miles   **Rank:** 20th
Population: 2,853,214   **Rank:** 23rd
Admission Date: November 11, 1889
                    Rank: 42nd

Major Sources of Income:

Forestry
  Douglas fir, ponderosa pine, hemlock, spruce

Manufacturing and Processing
  transportation equipment, lumber and wood products, food products

Agriculture and Livestock
  wheat, fruit, beef cattle and dairy products

Climate:

Western Washington has mild winters and summers cooled by ocean breezes. Summer temperatures average about 62 degrees. Heavy rainfall occurs on the ocean-facing slopes of the Olympics. Winters are wet and temperatures average about 40 degrees. Snow is confined for the most part to the high mountain regions. East of the Cascades, average temperatures range higher. Although there are heavy snows in the mountains, the valleys of central Washington are extremely dry with little snow or rain. Mid-summer temperatures often reach 90 degrees but the extremely dry air acts as a cooling agent.

Washington was once part of the vast Oregon Territory. Within its present-day boundaries, Washington is divided into two separate regions by the Cascade Range.

The western lowlands of the Puget Sound Valley lie between the foothills of the Cascades and the Pacific Ocean. Puget Sound itself is a series of deep channels, sunk below sea level long ago. These channels stretch for a hundred miles to the south. To the north the lowlands rise to meet the Olympic Mountains. The Puget Sound Valley is a region of moderate rainfall and mild climate.

Important Whens and Whats in the Making of Washington

1592 While searching for the Northwest Passage, Juan de Fuca, a Greek navigator serving the viceroy of Mexico, may have found the strait which now bears his name.

1792 Captain Robert Gray discovers and names the Columbia River, anchors, and trades with the Indians for furs.

1805 Lewis and Clark reach the mouth of the Columbia River and return to St. Lewis.

1810 The North West Fur Company establishes Spokane House, the first white settlement.

1819 The Florida Treaty with Spain gives the United States any and all rights claimed by Spain to the Oregon Country.

1836 The Whitmans and Spauldings arrive to build missions near Fort Walla-Walla, Lewiston, and Spokane.

1846 The United States and Great Britain fix the Canadian-Washington boundary.

1848 Oregon Territory, including all present-day Washington, is created.

1853 Washington Territory is created.

1889 Washington is admitted to the Union as the 42nd state.

East of the Cascades lies the high, arid Columbia Plateau, broken by deep river gorges or sheltered river valleys. The mighty Columbia River cuts south through the plateau then turns west to the Pacific, forming the boundary between Washington and Oregon.

Grand Coulee Dam reaches across the Columbia, storing up water for power and to irrigate a million acres of plateau and basin dry lands where rainfall is light. The dam forms the longest man-made lake in the world, 151-mile long Franklin Delano Roosevelt Lake.

The design and construction of vast irrigation projects, such as the Columbia River system, in addition to Washington's areas of heavy rainfall, help this state to produce a greater variety of agricultural products than any other state.

Famous for its apples, Washington also produces pears, peaches, cherries and berries.

Washington is a state of high wheat production and raises many other grains and vegetables. Flowers and vegetables are grown for seed.

Washington's regions of plentiful rainfall contain twelve per cent of all the growing timber in the country. As early as 1850 lumbermen came in ships from Maine and Canada bringing lumbering equipment and mill machinery with them to convert the vast stands of Douglas fir, pine and spruce into lumber and wood products.

Salmon, halibut and tuna netted by Washington's fishing fleets go to the fish packing and canning industries.

Flour milling, vegetable and fruit canning and drying, meat packing, ship building, atomic energy research for power, medicine and energy for industry, electronics industries and airplane manufacturing are part of Washington's industrial and processing life. Oil for the beginning of a fast-growing petroleum industry was found not long ago in Washington's Olympic Peninsula.

Seattle and Tacoma's harbors rank among the major Pacific ports and lead to Alaska, Hawaii and the Philippines.

Raw materials, transportation and research lead Washington to the future.

Glossary

basaltic (bȧ sôl′tĭk) like basalt—a dark-gray to black, dense to fine-grained igneous rock.

borax (bō′răks) a crystalline substance used as a cleansing agent.

carnivore (kär′nĭ vōr) an animal which eats flesh, such as a dog, cat, bear, seal, lion, etc.

coral (kŏr′ăl) the skeletons of tiny ocean animals, many of which, in solid and stony masses, make up tropical islands and reefs.

culture (kŭl′tūr) 1. a particular stage in the development of a civilization; 2. the characteristic features of such a stage.

drought (drout) 1. dryness; in need of rain; 2. a dry spell.

dynasty (dī′năs tĭ) the succession of kings of the same family; the continued lordship of a race of rulers.

erosion (ė rō′zhŭn) the wearing away of land by the action of water, ice, or wind.

eruption (ė rŭp′shŭn) a bursting or breaking out, as of ashes from a volcano.

eucalyptus (ū′kȧ lĭp tŭs) a timber tree from Australia which secretes gums and oils.

floe (flō) a large mass of ice floating on a body of water.

geologic time (jē′ȯ lŏj′ĭk) time established from scientific records of the structure, composition and history of the earth.

glacier (glā′shĕr) a field or body of ice which moves slowly down a valley toward the sea.

grouse (grous) a plump, strong bird with feathered legs and a plume, usually spotted with red-brown or other colors to help conceal it.

irrigation (ir ĭ gā′shŭn) the process of supplying water artificially to land by canals, ditches, etc.

koa (kō′ȧ) a Hawaiian timber tree with valuable, fine-grained wood.

lanai (lä nä′ė) a veranda or porch.

lei (lā′ė; lā) a Hawaiian wreath or ornamental headdress; may be made of leaves and flowers, feathers or ivory.

luau (lōō′ou) a Hawaiian feast for special occasions at which many special foods are served.

poi (pō′ė; poi) a native Hawaiian food prepared from the taro root which is pounded to a paste and allowed to ferment.

predator (prĕd'ȧ tēr) an animal which preys on other animals or destroys crops.

ptarmigan (tär'mĭ găn) various species of grouse of northern regions, having completely feathered feet.

pumice (pŭm'ĭs) a variety of volcanic glass, full of tiny cavities and very light.

rookery (rŏŏk'ĕr ĭ) the breeding place of birds or seals.

sediment (sĕd'ĭ mĕnt) the matter which settles to the bottom from a liquid; material left after water has receded.

semi-tropical (sĕm'ĭ trŏp'ĭ kȧl) having to do with the regions of the earth which are near the tropics, but which are not as hot as those near the equator.

sourdough (sour'dō') the name given to a Canadian or Alaskan explorer or prospector from the sour dough he usually carried to make bread.

taro (tä'rō) a plant grown throughout the tropics for its starchy, tuberous rootstocks. In other regions it is called elephant's-ear and is grown for ornament.

temperate (tĕm'pēr ĭt) moderate, mild; not hot or cold.

trade wind (trād wĭnd) a drying wind blowing almost continually in the same direction toward the equator from the east.

tropical (trŏp'ĭ kȧl) having to do with the tropics; temperatures as hot as those near the equator.

tundra (tŏŏn'drȧ; tŭn'drȧ) the level, treeless plains of northern arctic regions, continually frozen a foot or so below the surface.

volcanology (vŏl'kăn ŏl'ȯ jĭ) the study of volcanoes and their actions.

windward (wĭnd'wērd) the direction from which the wind blows; toward the wind.

Grateful acknowledgment is made to the following for the helpful information and materials furnished by them, used in the preparation of this book:

United States Department of the Interior, National Park Service; particularly, the National Parks of: Crater Lake, Hawaii, Lassen Volcanic, Mount McKinley; Mount Rainier, Olympic, Sequoia and Kings Canyon, Yosemite; and their respective managements.

United States Department of Commerce, Bureau of the Census, Field Services, Chicago, Illinois.

State of Alaska Department of Natural Resources, Division of Economic and Tourist Development, Tourist Section.

California State Chamber of Commerce.

All-Year Club of Southern California.

Californians, Incorporated.

Redwood Empire Association.

State of Hawaii Department of Economic Development.

Oregon State Highway Department.

Washington Department of Commerce and Economic Development.

International Visual Educational Services, Inc., Chicago, Illinois.

Index

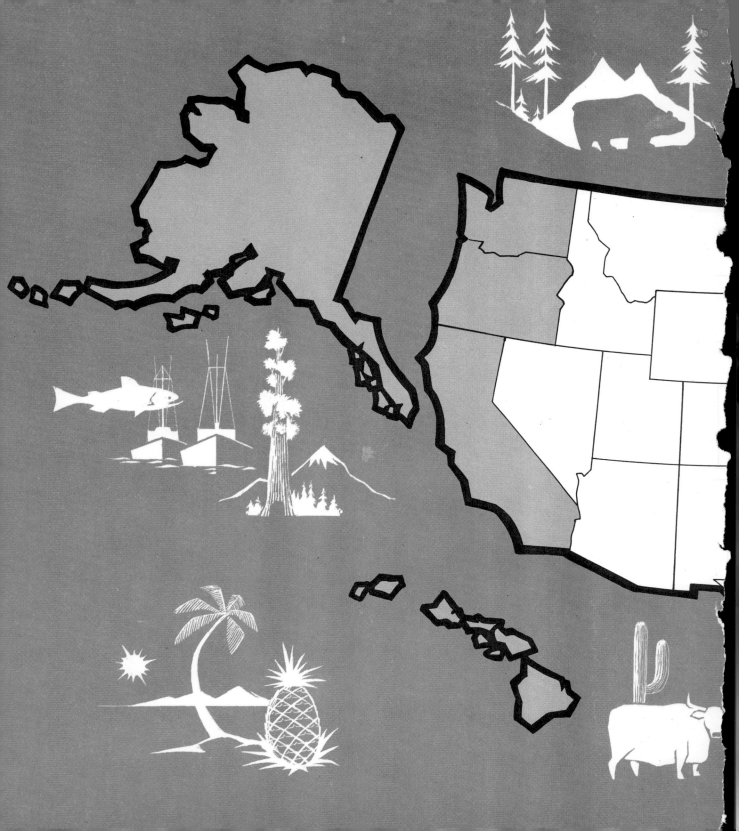

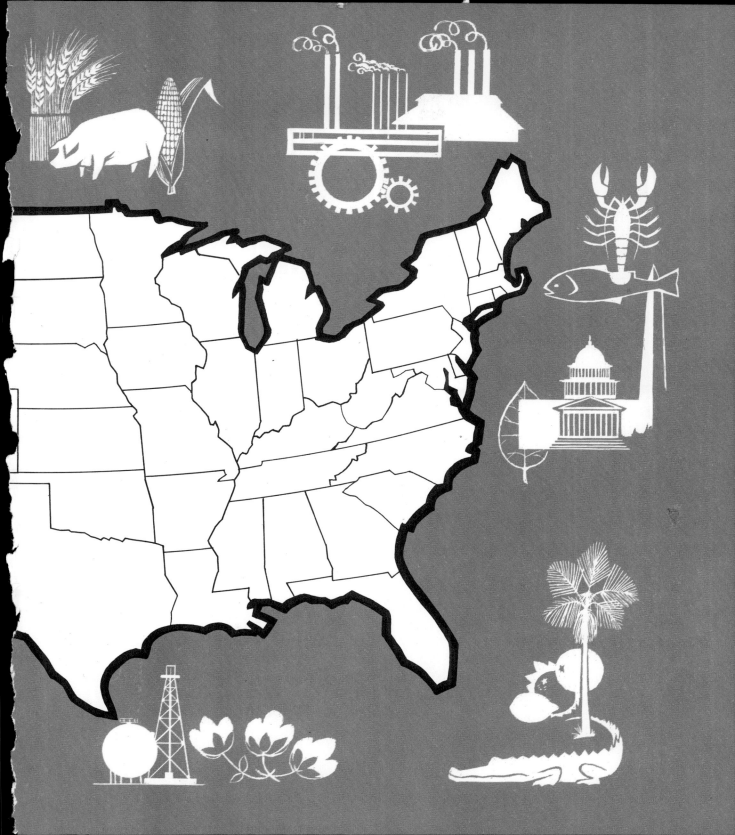